Dream Alaska: A Travel Preparation Guide.

Daniel Hunter

All rights reserved. No part of this publication may be reproduced, distributed, or transmitted in any form or by any means, including photocopying, recording, or other electronic or mechanical methods, without the prior written permission of the publisher, except in the case of brief quotations embodied in critical reviews and certain other noncommercial uses permitted by copyright law.

Copyright © (Daniel Hunter) (2023).

TABLE OF CONTENTS

Introduction — 7
1. Welcome to the Last Frontier: An Overview of Alaska — 8
2. When to Visit: Choosing the Best Season for Your Trip — 11
3. Planning Your Alaska Adventure: A Quick Guide — 15

Chapter 1: Essential Preparations — 19
4. Travel Documents and Permits — 19
5. Packing Tips for Alaska's Varied Climate — 21
6. Safety Precautions and Wildlife Awareness — 24

Chapter 2: Solo Traveler's Guide — 29
7. Embracing Solo Adventures in Alaska — 29
8. Accommodation Options for Solo Travelers — 32
9. Solo-Friendly Activities and Tours — 35
10. Dining Alone: Tips for Solo Diners — 38
11. Meeting Locals and Fellow Travelers — 41

Chapter 3: Family-Friendly Alaska — 45
12. Alaska with Kids: A Family-Focused Overview — 45
13. Family-Friendly Accommodations — 48
14. Kid-Friendly Activities and Attractions — 51
15. Dining with Children: Family Restaurants — 55
16. Tips for Smooth Family Travel — 58

Chapter 4: Romantic Getaways for Couples — 63
17. Romance in the Wilderness: An Alaska Experience — 63
18. Cozy Cabins and Romantic Lodges — 66
19. Couples' Adventure Activities — 68
20. Romantic Dining Spots — 71

21. Tips for a Memorable Couple's Retreat   74

Chapter 5: Exploring Alaska's Regions   79

22. Anchorage and the Southcentral Region   79

23. Denali National Park and the Interior   81

24. The Alaska Panhandle: Southeastern Adventures   84

25. Fairbanks and the Interior North   88

26. Discovering the Far North: The Arctic Region   91

27. Western Alaska: Off-the-Beaten-Path Treasures   94

Chapter 6: Outdoor Adventures   99

28. Hiking and Trekking in Alaska's Wilderness   99

29. Wildlife Encounters: Watching and Safety   103

30. Fishing and Boating in Alaska's Waters   106

31. Winter Wonderland: Activities in the Snow   109

32. Camping and RV Travel Tips   112

Chapter 7: Cultural Experiences   117

33. Alaska's Indigenous Cultures and History   117

34. Museums, Art, and Cultural Centers   119

35. Festivals and Events: Celebrating Alaska's Spirit   122

Chapter 8: Practical Information   127

36. Transportation Options in Alaska   127

37. Budgeting and Cost Considerations   130

38. Communication and Connectivity   133

39. Health and Safety Tips   136

40. Sustainable Travel in Alaska   139

Chapter 9: Itineraries and Sample Plans   143

41. One-Week Itinerary for a Family Adventure   143

42. Two-Week Solo Expedition	145
43. Romantic Escape in Alaska: a 5-Day Plan	147
44. Customizing Your Alaska Experience	149
Chapter 10: Resources and Contacts	**153**
45. Useful Websites and Apps	153
46. Emergency Contacts and Services	156
47. Travel Agencies and Tour Operators	159
Appendices	**165**
- Packing Checklist	165
- Wildlife Identification Guide	168
- Glossary of Alaskan Terms	172
- Recommended Reading and Films	175

Introduction

Welcome to the Last Frontier! Alaska, the largest and wildest state in the United States, beckons you to embark on an extraordinary adventure like no other. Nestled in the far reaches of North America, this vast land of towering mountains, pristine wilderness, and untamed wildlife offers a journey into the heart of natural beauty and rugged charm.

In this Alaska travel guide, we invite you to explore a land of endless possibilities, whether you're a solo adventurer seeking solitude, a family looking to create lasting memories, or a couple seeking a romantic escape. Alaska's diverse landscapes, rich cultural heritage, and unparalleled outdoor experiences promise something special for every traveler.

Discover the secrets of Denali National Park's majestic peaks, witness the magic of the Northern Lights dancing across Arctic skies, and immerse yourself in the vibrant cultures of Alaska's indigenous communities. Whether you're drawn to the thrill of outdoor adventure, the allure of wildlife encounters, or the serenity of remote cabins, Alaska's wonders await your exploration.

Join us as we navigate the icy waters of the Inside Passage, traverse vast tundra and rainforests, and uncover the hidden gems of Anchorage, Fairbanks, and beyond. This guide is your key to unlocking the treasures of Alaska, providing insights, tips, and recommendations to ensure your journey is as unforgettable as the state itself.

Prepare to be captivated by the pristine landscapes, inspired by the rich history, and enchanted by the warm hospitality of Alaskans. Your Alaska adventure begins here, where the call of the wild is only matched by the spirit of adventure. So, pack your bags and get ready to experience the awe-inspiring beauty and untamed wilderness of Alaska – the adventure of a lifetime awaits!

1. Welcome to the Last Frontier: An Overview of Alaska

Alaska, often referred to as "The Last Frontier," is a land of awe-inspiring wilderness, rugged landscapes, and unparalleled natural beauty. Located in the far northwest corner of North America, Alaska is the largest state in the United States, boasting immense glaciers, towering mountains, pristine fjords, and abundant wildlife.

Geography and Climate:

Alaska's geography is as diverse as it is stunning. From the icy shores of the Arctic Ocean to the temperate rainforests of the southeast, the state offers an array of ecosystems. The towering peaks of the Alaska Range, including Denali, North America's highest peak, dominate the interior, while coastal regions feature countless islands and the famous Inside Passage. The climate varies greatly, from subarctic and polar climates in the north to more temperate conditions in the south. Summer brings extended daylight, while winter offers opportunities for snow sports and the mesmerizing Northern Lights.

Wildlife and Natural Wonders:
Alaska is a wildlife enthusiast's dream. Grizzly bears, bald eagles, moose, and whales are just a few of the remarkable creatures that call this place home. The state's national parks, including Denali, Kenai Fjords, and Glacier Bay, protect these ecosystems and provide opportunities for wildlife viewing, hiking, and exploring some of the most impressive glaciers on the planet.

Outdoor Adventures:
For adventurers and outdoor enthusiasts, Alaska offers endless possibilities. Hiking, fishing, kayaking, and wildlife safaris are just a few of the

activities that allow travelers to immerse themselves in the pristine wilderness. Whether you're scaling a glacier, paddling through tranquil waters, or trying your hand at dog sledding, there's an adventure awaiting you.

Cultural Richness:
Alaska is not just about its natural wonders; it's also a place of rich cultural heritage. Indigenous cultures, such as the Alaska Natives, have lived here for thousands of years and have a profound connection to the land. Visitors have the opportunity to learn about their traditions, art, and history through museums, cultural centers, and interactions with local communities.

Getting Around:
Traveling in Alaska can be an adventure in itself. While road networks connect major cities like Anchorage and Fairbanks, many remote areas are accessible only by small planes or boats. Cruises along the Inside Passage offer a unique way to explore the coastal regions, while scenic train rides showcase the breathtaking landscapes of the interior.

Alaska is a place of unparalleled natural beauty and adventure, offering a once-in-a-lifetime experience for travelers of all kinds. Whether you seek solitude in the wilderness, want to witness the spectacle of the Northern Lights, or simply want to explore its diverse landscapes, Alaska promises an unforgettable journey into the heart of the wild.

2. When to Visit: Choosing the Best Season for Your Trip

Alaska's allure lies not only in its stunning landscapes but also in its ever-changing seasons, each offering a unique set of experiences. When planning your trip to the Last Frontier, it's crucial to consider the time of year that aligns with your interests and the type of adventure you seek. Alaska's seasons can be roughly categorized into four distinct periods, each with its own charm and activities.

1. Summer (June to August): The Season of Abundance

Summer is the most popular time to visit Alaska, and for good reason. This is when the state experiences its mildest weather, with temperatures ranging from 50°F to 70°F (10°C to 25°C) in most regions. During this season:

- Wildlife Abounds: Summer is prime wildlife viewing time. You can witness bears catching salmon, eagles soaring, and whales breaching along the coast.

- Midnight Sun: In northern Alaska, you can experience the phenomenon of the midnight sun, with 24 hours of daylight. This allows for extended exploration and outdoor activities.

- Vibrant Flora: Alaska's wilderness bursts into life with colorful wildflowers and lush vegetation. Hiking and camping enthusiasts will be in their element.

- Festivals and Events: Numerous cultural festivals and outdoor events take place during summer, offering a chance to immerse yourself in local culture.

2. Fall (September to November): The Season of Change

Fall in Alaska is a time of transition, marked by cooler temperatures and shorter days. However, this season has its own unique appeal:

- Spectacular Foliage: The changing colors of the leaves create a stunning backdrop for your travels, especially in the interior and southcentral regions.

- Fewer Crowds: As the summer tourists disperse, you'll find fewer crowds at popular attractions, making it a peaceful time to explore.

- Northern Lights: As the nights grow longer, you might catch a glimpse of the mesmerizing Northern Lights, especially in the far north.

3. Winter (December to February): The Season of Snow

Winter in Alaska is synonymous with snow and sub-zero temperatures. If you're a fan of winter sports and unique experiences, this is the time to visit:

- A Winter Wonderland: Alaska's landscape transforms into a pristine snowy wonderland, perfect for activities like skiing, dog sledding, and ice fishing.

- Aurora Borealis: The long nights provide ample opportunities to witness the enchanting Northern Lights dance across the sky.

- Cozy Cabins: Snuggle up in cozy cabins and lodges, enjoying the warmth of a crackling fire and the serenity of the winter landscape.

4. Spring (March to May): The Season of Rebirth

Spring in Alaska is a time of awakening, as the snow begins to melt and the days grow longer. It's a transitional season with its own unique allure:

- Migratory Birds: Spring is the season when migratory birds return to Alaska. Birdwatchers will be treated to a symphony of bird songs.

- Wilderness Whitewater: As the snow melts, rivers become lively with whitewater rapids, attracting kayakers and rafters seeking an adrenaline rush.

- Emerging Wildlife: Witness the renewal of wildlife as animals emerge from hibernation and the landscape transforms.

Ultimately, the best time to visit Alaska depends on your interests and the experiences you seek. Whether you're drawn to the endless daylight of summer, the snowy adventures of winter, or the peacefulness of fall and spring, Alaska offers something extraordinary year-round. Plan your trip according to your preferences, and you'll undoubtedly discover the magic of this incredible destination.

3. Planning Your Alaska Adventure: A Quick Guide

Planning a trip to Alaska requires careful consideration to make the most of your adventure in this vast and diverse state. Here's a quick guide to help you get started on your Alaska journey.

1. Setting Expectations:
   - Understand that Alaska is enormous, and you won't see it all in one trip. Focus on specific regions or activities that interest you the most.

2. Choosing the Right Time:
   - Determine the best time to visit based on your interests. Summer (June to August) offers long daylight hours, while winter (December to March) is ideal for aurora viewing and winter sports.

3. Duration of Stay:
   - Decide how long you can stay. Alaska's size makes it challenging to explore comprehensively in a short time, so prioritize your must-see places.

4. Budgeting:
   - Calculate your budget, considering transportation, accommodation, activities, and meals. Alaska can be expensive, but there are options for various budgets.

5. Transportation:
   - Choose your mode of transportation, whether it's flying into major cities like Anchorage or Fairbanks or embarking on a cruise to explore coastal regions.

6. Accommodation:
   - Research and book accommodation in advance, especially during the peak tourist season. Options range from hotels and lodges to cabins and campgrounds.

7. Activities and Tours:
   - Identify the activities and tours that interest you, such as hiking, wildlife viewing, fishing, or cultural experiences. Book popular tours ahead of time.

8. Wildlife and Safety:
   - Learn about Alaska's wildlife and safety precautions. Carry bear spray, be aware of wildlife encounters, and follow Leave No Trace principles.

9. Weather and Clothing:

- Pack clothing suitable for Alaska's ever-changing weather. Layering is key, and don't forget rain gear and sturdy hiking boots.

10. Travel Insurance:
   - Consider travel insurance that covers unexpected events, such as flight cancellations or medical emergencies in remote areas.

11. Itinerary Planning:
   - Create a rough itinerary, outlining which places you want to visit and the activities you'd like to experience. Be flexible to adapt to weather and other factors.

12. Permits and Regulations:
   - Check if any permits or park passes are required for the areas you plan to visit, especially if you intend to hike or camp in national parks.

13. Local Insights:
   - Seek advice from locals, tour operators, or fellow travelers. They can provide valuable tips and hidden gems.

14. Leave No Trace:

- Embrace responsible travel by following Leave No Trace principles to preserve the pristine wilderness of Alaska.

15. Documentation:
   - Ensure you have all necessary travel documents, including your ID, passport, driver's license, and any permits or reservations.

Remember, Alaska offers a wide range of experiences, from rugged wilderness adventures to cultural encounters and scenic drives. Tailor your trip to your interests, and don't rush—take the time to savor the breathtaking landscapes and unique culture that Alaska has to offer.

Chapter 1: Essential Preparations

4. Travel Documents and Permits

Before embarking on your Alaska adventure, it's essential to ensure you have all the necessary travel documents and permits in order. This section will guide you through the paperwork you'll need to explore the Last Frontier with ease.

1. Passport and Identification:
   - If you're a U.S. citizen traveling to Alaska from another state, you won't need a passport or visa, as Alaska is part of the United States. A valid government-issued photo ID, such as a driver's license, should suffice for domestic travel.
   - However, if you're an international traveler, make sure to carry your passport and any required visas for entry into the United States.

2. Proof of Citizenship for Cruises:
   - If your Alaska journey includes a cruise that departs or returns to a Canadian port (common for cruises in Southeast Alaska), you'll need to carry your passport, as Canadian immigration requirements may apply.

3. Wildlife Viewing Permits:

- Alaska boasts incredible wildlife, including bears, eagles, and marine life. To ensure responsible wildlife viewing, you may need permits, particularly if you plan to visit specific wildlife refuges or protected areas. Check with the Alaska Department of Fish and Game or the National Park Service for permit requirements.

4. Fishing Licenses:
   - If you're planning to go fishing during your trip, be aware that Alaska has strict fishing regulations. You'll likely need a fishing license, which can be obtained online or at various local vendors.

5. National Park Passes:
   - Alaska is home to several national parks and preserves, including Denali, Katmai, and Glacier Bay. Purchasing an America the Beautiful Pass can be a cost-effective option if you plan to visit multiple national parks during your trip.

6. Remote Area Permits:
   - If you intend to explore more remote areas, such as the Arctic or certain wilderness regions, you might require additional permits. These permits help authorities manage visitor impact on the delicate ecosystems of these pristine areas.

7. Customs Declarations:
   - If you're traveling to Alaska from another country, be prepared to fill out customs declarations forms upon arrival in the United States. Ensure you're aware of what items are allowed and prohibited to avoid any delays.

8. Vehicle Documentation:
   - If you're planning a road trip in Alaska, make sure your vehicle registration and insurance are up to date. If you're renting a vehicle, confirm that the rental company provides the necessary documents.

Always check the most recent travel and entry requirements, as regulations can change. It's a good practice to keep physical and digital copies of your important travel documents and permits to avoid any unforeseen complications during your Alaskan adventure. With the right paperwork in hand, you'll be ready to explore this incredible wilderness with peace of mind.

5. Packing Tips for Alaska's Varied Climate

One of the unique aspects of traveling to Alaska is the incredible diversity in its climate. From icy glaciers to temperate rainforests, and arctic tundras to coastal plains, Alaska offers a wide range of environments. To ensure you're well-prepared for your trip, packing appropriately is key. Here are some essential packing tips to navigate Alaska's varied climate with ease.

1. Layering is Key:

Alaska's weather can change rapidly, so packing versatile clothing is essential. Dressing in layers allows you to adapt to shifting temperatures throughout the day. Start with a moisture-wicking base layer to keep you dry, add insulating layers for warmth, and finish with a waterproof and windproof outer shell.

2. Waterproof Gear:

Rain is a frequent companion in certain regions, especially along the coast and in the southeast. Bring a high-quality waterproof jacket and pants to stay dry during rainy spells. Additionally, waterproof hiking boots are a must for outdoor activities.

3. Warm Accessories:

Even in summer, nights in Alaska can be quite chilly. Don't forget to pack warm accessories like gloves, a hat, and a scarf. For colder seasons, consider thermal undergarments and insulated gloves.

4. Mosquito Protection:

In the summer, Alaska's state bird may as well be the mosquito! Bring insect repellent and a head net to fend off these persistent pests when exploring the great outdoors.

5. Binoculars and Cameras:

Alaska's stunning landscapes and wildlife call for good optics. Be sure to pack binoculars and a camera with extra batteries and memory cards to capture those unforgettable moments.

6. Bear Safety Gear:

If you plan on hiking in bear country, pack bear spray and educate yourself on bear safety. Bear bells and bear-resistant food containers are also advisable.

7. Electronics and Charging:

Keep your devices charged as power sources can be scarce in remote areas. Consider a portable power bank to keep your smartphone, camera, and other gadgets ready for action.

8. Medications and First Aid:

If you require prescription medications, ensure you have an ample supply for the duration of your trip. A basic first-aid kit is also a wise addition to your packing list.

9. Casual and Dressier Attire:
While Alaska is known for its rugged outdoors, there are occasions when you may want to dress up a bit. Include some casual and dressier attire for evenings out or special occasions.

10. Backpack:
A comfortable and sturdy backpack is essential for carrying your essentials while exploring. Choose one with good back support, especially for longer hikes.

Remember, your packing list may vary depending on the specific region and time of year you plan to visit. Always check the weather forecast for your destination and adjust your packing accordingly. By following these tips, you'll be well-prepared to embrace the diverse climate of Alaska and make the most of your adventure.

6. Safety Precautions and Wildlife Awareness

Alaska's pristine wilderness is undoubtedly one of its greatest attractions, but it also comes with inherent risks and challenges. Whether you're a solo traveler, a family, or a couple, safety should always be a top priority during your Alaskan adventure. Additionally, understanding and respecting the diverse wildlife that calls this state home is crucial for your own safety and the preservation of the environment.

Safety Precautions:

1. Weather Awareness: Alaska's weather can be unpredictable. Check forecasts regularly and be prepared for sudden changes in temperature and conditions, especially if you plan to explore remote areas.

2. Wilderness Survival Skills: Familiarize yourself with basic survival skills such as building a shelter, making a fire, and purifying water. These skills can be vital in emergencies.

3. Navigation Tools: Carry a map, GPS, or compass, especially if you're venturing into the backcountry. Trails and landmarks may not always be well-marked.

4. Emergency Communication: Invest in a satellite phone or locator beacon, especially in areas with

limited cell phone coverage. Inform someone of your itinerary and expected return time.

5. Bear Safety: Alaska is home to both black bears and grizzly bears. Learn about bear behavior, carry bear spray, make noise while hiking to alert bears of your presence, and know how to react in case of a bear encounter.

6. Water Safety: If you plan to engage in water activities, wear appropriate safety gear like life jackets, and be aware of cold water hazards.

Wildlife Awareness:

1. Maintain Distance: Observe wildlife from a safe and respectful distance. Do not approach or feed them. This includes bears, moose, eagles, and other creatures.

2. Bear-Proof Food Storage: When camping, store food securely in bear-resistant containers or hang it in bear bags to avoid attracting bears to your campsite.

3. Moose Safety: Moose can be unpredictable and protective of their young. Give them plenty of space, especially if you encounter a moose with calves.

4. Marine Wildlife: If you go whale watching or boating, be cautious around marine mammals. Keep a safe distance to avoid disturbing them.

5. Bird Nesting Areas: Alaska is a crucial nesting area for many seabirds. Respect nesting sites and keep a distance to avoid causing stress to these birds.

6. Leave No Trace: Follow the principles of Leave No Trace to minimize your impact on the environment and wildlife. Pack out all trash and waste.

7. Fishing Ethics: If you plan to fish, learn and adhere to local fishing regulations to protect fish populations and their habitats.

Alaska's natural beauty and wildlife encounters are unparalleled, but they come with responsibilities. By being well-prepared, practicing safety precautions, and respecting the wildlife, you can enjoy a safe and enriching Alaskan experience while contributing to the preservation of this remarkable ecosystem.

Chapter 2: Solo Traveler's Guide

7. Embracing Solo Adventures in Alaska

Alaska, often referred to as "The Last Frontier," offers a unique and exhilarating experience for solo travelers. Embracing solo adventures in Alaska can be a transformative journey filled with breathtaking landscapes, wildlife encounters, and the freedom to explore at your own pace. In this section of our Alaska travel guide, we'll delve into what makes solo travel in Alaska so special and provide you with tips for an unforgettable journey.

Why Choose Solo Travel in Alaska?

1. Personal Growth: Solo travel allows you to step out of your comfort zone and discover your inner strengths. Alaska's rugged terrain and remote wilderness provide the perfect backdrop for personal growth and self-discovery.

2. Complete Freedom: When traveling alone, you have the freedom to choose your own itinerary, make spontaneous decisions, and immerse yourself in the wilderness without compromise. Alaska's vast landscapes are yours to explore on your terms.

3. Connection with Nature: Alaska's pristine wilderness, from towering mountains to icy glaciers and dense forests, beckons you to connect with nature in a profound way. Solo travelers often find solace and inspiration in the natural beauty that surrounds them.

4. Wildlife Encounters: Alaska is home to a diverse array of wildlife, including bears, moose, whales, and bald eagles. Solo travelers can relish the opportunity to observe these creatures in their natural habitat, fostering a deep appreciation for the animal kingdom.

Tips for Solo Travelers in Alaska

1. Safety First: While Alaska is generally safe for travelers, it's essential to be well-prepared. Inform someone of your travel plans, carry bear spray, and stay informed about local wildlife and safety guidelines.

2. Pack Smart: Alaska's weather can be unpredictable, so pack layers, rain gear, and sturdy footwear. Don't forget essentials like a first aid kit, GPS or maps, and a reliable communication device.

3. Connect with Locals: Alaskans are known for their friendliness and hospitality. Engage with locals to gain valuable insights into the region, discover hidden gems, and even make new friends along the way.

4. Explore National Parks: Alaska boasts incredible national parks like Denali, Katmai, and Kenai Fjords. These parks offer well-maintained trails and visitor centers, making them ideal for solo exploration.

5. Tours and Excursions: Consider joining guided tours or excursions for activities like wildlife watching, glacier hiking, or kayaking. These experiences provide both safety and opportunities to meet fellow adventurers.

6. Photography Paradise: Alaska is a photographer's dream. Capture the mesmerizing landscapes and wildlife encounters, creating lasting memories of your solo adventure.

Embracing solo adventures in Alaska is a thrilling and rewarding experience that allows you to discover the untamed beauty of this remarkable state while gaining a deeper understanding of yourself. Whether you're hiking through pristine wilderness, watching grizzlies catching salmon, or gazing in wonder at the Northern Lights, Alaska's wilderness welcomes those who dare to explore it alone. So, pack your bags, set out on your own Alaskan odyssey, and embrace the solitude and grandeur that await you.

8. Accommodation Options for Solo Travelers

When embarking on a solo adventure in Alaska, choosing the right accommodation can significantly enhance your experience. Alaska offers a diverse range of options to suit various preferences and budgets. Here are some suggestions tailored to solo travelers:

1. Hostels and Budget Lodges:
   - Affordable and Social: Hostels in cities like Anchorage and Juneau provide budget-friendly accommodation with dormitory-style rooms. They are great for meeting fellow travelers and sharing experiences.
   - Local Flavor: Look for locally-owned budget lodges and cabins, especially in smaller towns. They offer a more authentic Alaskan experience without breaking the bank.

2. Bed and Breakfasts (B&Bs):

- Personalized Hospitality: B&Bs are excellent for solo travelers seeking a cozy, homey atmosphere. You'll often have the chance to connect with local hosts who can provide insider tips on the area.

3. Camping and RV Parks:
  - Nature Immersion: Alaska's vast wilderness is a camping enthusiast's paradise. Consider camping in state parks, national forests, or private campgrounds. It's a fantastic way to immerse yourself in the pristine natural surroundings.

4. Solo-Friendly Hotels:
  - Convenience and Comfort: If you prefer the amenities of hotels, look for those with solo traveler-friendly features like communal spaces, social events, and smaller room options.

5. Wilderness Cabins:
  - Remote Retreats: For a truly unique experience, rent a wilderness cabin in a remote area. These rustic cabins offer solitude and the chance to disconnect from the world while enjoying Alaska's breathtaking landscapes.

6. Airbnb and Vacation Rentals:
  - Local Living: Airbnb and vacation rentals can be ideal for solo travelers looking for a home away

from home. You can find a wide range of options, from cozy cabins to city apartments.

7. Lodges in National Parks:
   - Unparalleled Scenery: If your Alaska adventure includes exploring national parks like Denali or Glacier Bay, consider staying in lodges within the parks. They offer proximity to incredible natural beauty.

8. Floating Lodges and Cruise Ships:
   - Marine Adventures: If you want to experience Alaska's coastal regions, consider staying on a cruise ship or a floating lodge. These options allow you to explore the coastline while enjoying comfortable accommodations.

Tips for Solo Travelers:
- Make reservations in advance, especially during peak tourist seasons.
- Join group tours and activities to meet fellow travelers.
- Practice bear safety and wildlife awareness when staying in remote areas.
- Utilize travel forums and social media groups to connect with other solo travelers and get recommendations.

- Always inform someone about your travel plans and expected return time, especially if you're venturing into remote areas.

Alaska's accommodation options for solo travelers are as diverse as its landscapes. Whether you crave social interactions or solitude, there's a perfect lodging choice to complement your solo journey in the Last Frontier.

9. Solo-Friendly Activities and Tours

Alaska, with its vast and pristine wilderness, offers numerous opportunities for solo travelers to embark on unique adventures. Whether you're seeking solitude in nature or looking to connect with fellow explorers, there's something for every solo adventurer in the Last Frontier.

1. Hiking and Trekking: Alaska boasts an extensive network of hiking trails, from easy day hikes to challenging multi-day treks. Solo hikers can explore the stunning landscapes of Denali National Park, the Chugach Mountains, or the Kenai Peninsula. Remember to check trail conditions, carry bear safety gear, and let someone know your plans before setting out.

2. Wildlife Viewing: Alaska is a paradise for wildlife enthusiasts. Join guided wildlife tours in places like Katmai National Park or Kodiak Island to witness grizzly bears in their natural habitat. Alternatively, embark on a self-guided wildlife adventure in parks and refuges across the state.

3. Sea Kayaking: Paddle through Alaska's pristine waters on a solo sea kayaking expedition. Explore coastal fjords, glacier-carved bays, and remote islands. Rentals and guided tours are available in places like Resurrection Bay near Seward or Glacier Bay National Park.

4. Northern Lights Viewing: Witnessing the aurora borealis is a bucket-list experience. Head to Fairbanks or other northern regions during the winter months for a chance to see this dazzling natural phenomenon. Many lodges and tours cater to solo travelers eager to chase the lights.

5. Alaska Railroad Journeys: Traveling by train is a fantastic way to see Alaska's scenic beauty. The Alaska Railroad offers various routes, including the renowned Denali Star route. Solo travelers can enjoy the scenery and meet fellow passengers during the journey.

6. Photography Expeditions: If you're a photography enthusiast, consider joining specialized photography tours. These tours take you to prime locations for capturing Alaska's stunning landscapes, wildlife, and northern lights. Some operators even provide equipment for rent.

7. Fishing Adventures: Alaska is a paradise for anglers. Join guided fishing charters or try your luck with a fly rod in pristine rivers and streams. Whether you're into salmon, halibut, or trout, there's a fishing adventure waiting for you.

8. Cultural Experiences: Connect with Alaska's indigenous cultures through cultural tours and visits to heritage centers. Learn about the traditions, art, and history of Alaska's Native peoples. These experiences provide insight into the rich tapestry of the state's heritage.

9. Adventure Cruises: Alaska's coastline is dotted with fjords, glaciers, and remote islands. Solo travelers can embark on small ship cruises, allowing for an intimate and adventurous exploration of Alaska's coastal wonders.

10. Flightseeing Tours: Take to the skies on a flightseeing tour and witness Alaska's grandeur

from above. Solo travelers can join group flights or opt for private tours to get a bird's-eye view of glaciers, mountains, and wildlife.

Remember to plan ahead, make reservations when necessary, and be prepared for the unpredictable Alaskan weather. Alaska's natural beauty and adventure await solo travelers seeking a memorable and rewarding journey in this remarkable wilderness.

10. Dining Alone: Tips for Solo Diners

Alaska's vast and pristine landscapes may be the primary draw for travelers, but its culinary scene is equally enticing. For solo travelers, dining alone in Alaska can be a delightful experience that allows you to savor the flavors of the Last Frontier at your own pace. Here are some tips to make the most of your solo dining adventures in Alaska.

1. Embrace the Alaskan Cuisine: Alaska offers a unique culinary landscape influenced by its indigenous cultures, fresh seafood, and locally sourced ingredients. Don't miss the chance to try regional specialties like wild salmon, king crab, reindeer sausage, and foraged berries. Many

restaurants take pride in showcasing these local flavors on their menus.

2. Make Reservations: While Alaska is known for its wilderness, its dining establishments can get busy, especially during the tourist season. To secure a table for one, it's advisable to make reservations, especially at popular restaurants. This ensures you won't have to wait long for a seat.

3. Opt for Counter Seating: Solo diners often find comfort in sitting at the counter or bar. Not only does this provide a front-row view of the culinary action, but it also makes it easier to strike up conversations with chefs or fellow patrons. You might even get some insider recommendations.

4. Timing Matters: Consider dining during off-peak hours if you prefer a quieter, more relaxed atmosphere. Early dinners or late lunches can be excellent choices for solo travelers seeking a more intimate dining experience.

5. Bring a Good Book or Device: Dining alone offers a chance for quiet reflection or entertainment. Bring a book, tablet, or smartphone to keep yourself engaged while you enjoy your meal. Some restaurants also provide free Wi-Fi.

6. Engage with Locals: Alaskans are known for their friendliness and warmth. Don't hesitate to strike up a conversation with locals or fellow travelers sitting nearby. You might learn about hidden gems or receive valuable travel tips.

7. Ask for Recommendations: Servers and restaurant staff are often the best sources of local food knowledge. Don't hesitate to ask for recommendations or off-menu specials. They can guide you to dishes that are particularly fresh or unique that day.

8. Explore Street Food and Food Trucks: Alaska's street food scene is burgeoning, and food trucks offer an excellent opportunity to sample a variety of local dishes quickly. From reindeer hot dogs to halibut tacos, these mobile eateries provide a taste of Alaskan flavors on the go.

9. Practice Responsible Dining: Alaska takes sustainability seriously. Support eco-friendly dining practices by choosing restaurants that prioritize local, organic, and sustainably sourced ingredients. It's a great way to respect the state's natural beauty.

10. Enjoy the Scenic Views: Many restaurants in Alaska boast stunning views of glaciers, mountains, or waterways. Take advantage of these scenic dining spots to make your meal even more memorable.

Dining alone in Alaska can be a rewarding experience that allows you to savor the region's unique flavors and connect with its friendly residents. Whether you're indulging in seafood delicacies or enjoying a simple meal, solo dining can be a delicious adventure in the Last Frontier.

11. *Meeting Locals and Fellow Travelers*

One of the most enriching aspects of solo travel in Alaska is the opportunity to connect with both locals and fellow travelers who share your passion for adventure. The Last Frontier is renowned for its warm and welcoming community, and striking up conversations with the people you encounter can be an unforgettable part of your journey.

1. Embrace the Alaskan Hospitality

Alaskans are known for their friendly and welcoming nature. Don't hesitate to strike up a conversation with a local at a café, while hiking, or during a visit to a cultural center. You'll find that many Alaskans are more than happy to share their stories, recommend hidden gems, and even invite you to experience their way of life.

2. Join Group Activities

Participating in group activities and tours can be an excellent way to meet fellow travelers who share your interests. Whether it's a guided wilderness hike, a wildlife-watching excursion, or a kayaking adventure, these activities provide a natural platform for forming connections.

3. Stay in Social Accommodations

Consider booking accommodations known for their social atmosphere, such as hostels, lodges, or guesthouses. Many of these places organize communal meals, bonfires, or group outings, making it easy to meet other travelers from around the world.

4. Attend Local Events and Festivals

Check out the local event calendar for festivals, fairs, and community gatherings. These events often offer a glimpse into Alaska's culture and provide opportunities to interact with locals who are proud to showcase their traditions.

5. Use Social Media and Online Forums

Before your trip, join travel forums, Facebook groups, or other online communities dedicated to Alaska travel. You can connect with like-minded travelers, ask for advice, and even arrange meetups once you're in the state.

6. Respect the Environment and Cultures

While making connections is a rewarding aspect of solo travel, it's important to approach interactions with respect for the local environment and indigenous cultures. Alaska's natural beauty and heritage are precious, so always follow leave-no-trace principles and be culturally sensitive in your interactions.

7. Share Stories and Experiences

One of the joys of solo travel is having unique stories to share. As you meet fellow travelers and locals, swap tales of your adventures and listen to theirs. You'll find that these shared moments create lasting bonds and friendships.

8. Seek Out Local Cuisine

Food is a universal language, and Alaska boasts a diverse culinary scene influenced by its indigenous cultures and international visitors. Dining at local restaurants and food markets is an excellent way to strike up conversations and get insider tips on where to explore next.

Meeting locals and fellow travelers in Alaska can transform your solo adventure into a rich tapestry of shared experiences and meaningful connections. Embrace the openness of the Alaskan community, and you're bound to create memories that will last a lifetime.

Chapter 3: Family-Friendly Alaska

12. Alaska with Kids: A Family-Focused Overview

Alaska isn't just a destination for adventure seekers and couples; it's also a fantastic place for families with children to embark on unforgettable journeys. From its stunning natural beauty to its diverse wildlife and interactive cultural experiences, Alaska offers a wide range of family-friendly activities and attractions. In this part, we'll provide a family-focused overview of what Alaska has to offer.

1. Wildlife Encounters: Alaska's wilderness is teeming with wildlife, and kids will be captivated by the chance to see bears, moose, bald eagles, and whales in their natural habitats. Consider visiting the Alaska Wildlife Conservation Center or taking a wildlife cruise to get up close and personal with these magnificent creatures while ensuring your family's safety.

2. National Parks and Nature Reserves: Alaska is home to several national parks, including Denali National Park and Kenai Fjords National Park, where families can explore rugged landscapes, hike on kid-friendly trails, and learn about the

environment through visitor centers and ranger programs.

3. Outdoor Adventures: Depending on the season, engage in a variety of outdoor activities such as hiking, kayaking, and fishing. Many tour operators offer family-friendly options, and local guides can provide valuable insights into the region's natural wonders.

4. Hands-On Learning: Alaska is a living classroom for curious kids. Visit museums, like the Anchorage Museum, to discover the state's history and culture. Interactive exhibits and workshops are often available, making learning engaging and fun.

5. Cultural Experiences: Alaska's indigenous cultures have rich traditions and stories to share. Attend a native dance performance or participate in cultural workshops to gain a deeper appreciation of Alaska's heritage.

6. Kid-Friendly Accommodations: Many lodges and resorts in Alaska are family-friendly, offering amenities like family suites, game rooms, and outdoor play areas. Consider staying in a wilderness lodge to immerse your family in Alaska's natural surroundings.

7. Family Restaurants: Alaska's culinary scene isn't just for adults. You'll find restaurants that cater to young palates with kid's menus and casual dining options, ensuring that even picky eaters will have satisfying meals.

8. Safety First: While exploring Alaska's wilderness, always prioritize safety. Be bear aware, dress appropriately for the weather, and have emergency supplies on hand. It's essential to teach your children about the importance of respecting nature and wildlife.

9. Planning Your Itinerary: Create a well-balanced itinerary that includes a mix of outdoor adventures, cultural experiences, and downtime. Alaska's vast size can make travel between destinations time-consuming, so plan accordingly to avoid overexertion.

10. Unforgettable Memories: Alaska offers endless opportunities for family bonding and creating lasting memories. Encourage your kids to keep a journal, take photos, and actively participate in the planning process to make this journey uniquely theirs.

Alaska with kids can be an enriching and awe-inspiring experience. Whether your family is spotting grizzlies in the wilderness, exploring glaciers, or learning about native cultures, the Last Frontier offers something for every member of your family to cherish for a lifetime.

13. Family-Friendly Accommodations

When planning a family vacation in Alaska, choosing the right accommodations can make all the difference in ensuring a comfortable and enjoyable stay. Alaska offers a wide range of family-friendly lodging options, from cozy cabins nestled in the wilderness to family-oriented resorts with plenty of amenities. Here, we'll explore some of the top choices for family accommodations in various regions of Alaska.

Anchorage and the Southcentral Region

1. Family-Friendly Hotels: In Anchorage, you'll find numerous hotels that cater to families, offering spacious rooms, kid-friendly amenities, and easy access to the city's attractions.

2. Cabin Retreats: Consider renting a cabin in the Chugach State Park area, where your family can

enjoy the tranquility of nature while still being close to urban conveniences.

Denali National Park and the Interior

3. Lodges Inside Denali: Opt for accommodations inside Denali National Park, such as the Denali Princess Wilderness Lodge or the McKinley Chalet Resort, for an immersive wilderness experience.

4. Family Campgrounds: If your family enjoys camping, there are campgrounds in the Denali area that offer both tent and RV sites.

The Alaska Panhandle: Southeastern Adventures

5. Family Resorts: In places like Juneau or Sitka, look for family-oriented resorts with amenities like swimming pools, on-site dining, and organized activities for kids.

6. Vacation Rentals: Consider booking a vacation rental home or condo in towns like Ketchikan or Skagway for a more homey atmosphere.

Fairbanks and the Interior North

7. Cozy Cabins: Embrace the northern spirit by staying in a cozy log cabin in Fairbanks or surrounding areas. Many of these cabins come equipped with kitchens for family meal preparation.

8. Hotels with Aurora Views: If you're hoping to catch the Northern Lights, choose a hotel outside of Fairbanks with excellent aurora viewing opportunities.

Western Alaska: Off-the-Beaten-Path Treasures

9. Remote Wilderness Lodges: For a truly unique experience, consider staying at one of the remote wilderness lodges in Western Alaska. These lodges often offer guided activities like wildlife viewing and fishing.

10. Family-Friendly Inns: In towns like Nome or Bethel, look for family-friendly inns or bed and breakfasts that can provide a more personalized experience.

General Tips for Family Accommodations:

- Book Early: Alaska can get busy during peak tourist seasons, so it's wise to book your accommodations well in advance.

- Check Amenities: Ensure that the accommodations you choose have family-friendly amenities like cribs, high chairs, and kid's menus.

- Safety First: If you're traveling with young children, inquire about safety measures in place, such as childproofing options or room layouts.

- Ask Locals: Don't hesitate to ask locals or other travelers for recommendations on family-friendly places to stay. Their insights can be invaluable.

Choosing the right family-friendly accommodations in Alaska can help create lasting memories for your loved ones. Whether you're looking for a wilderness retreat, a seaside resort, or a city hotel, Alaska has options that cater to families of all sizes and interests.

14. Kid-Friendly Activities and Attractions

Alaska isn't just a destination for adventure-seeking adults; it's also a fantastic place for families with kids. In this part, we'll explore the wide range of kid-friendly activities and attractions that will make your family vacation in Alaska unforgettable.

1. Alaska Wildlife Conservation Center

Located in Portage, the Alaska Wildlife Conservation Center offers a unique opportunity for children to see native Alaskan wildlife up close. Kids will be thrilled to observe grizzly bears, moose, caribou, and other animals in a safe and natural environment. Educational programs and guided tours make this a fun and informative stop for the whole family.

2. Alaska SeaLife Center

Seward is home to the Alaska SeaLife Center, an interactive marine science facility that's perfect for curious young minds. Children can marvel at sea otters, puffins, harbor seals, and more. Interactive exhibits and touch tanks provide hands-on learning experiences, making it an educational adventure for kids of all ages.

3. Denali National Park Junior Ranger Program

Denali National Park offers a Junior Ranger program designed to engage children in the wonders of nature. Kids can complete age-appropriate activities and attend ranger-led programs to earn their Junior Ranger badges. It's a great way for kids to learn about Alaska's wilderness while having fun.

4. Alaska Native Heritage Center

Anchorage's Alaska Native Heritage Center introduces families to the rich cultures and traditions of Alaska's indigenous peoples. Kids can participate in activities like traditional dance, storytelling, and arts and crafts. It's an eye-opening experience that fosters cultural understanding.

5. Gold Rush Towns and Panning

Take your family back in time to the days of the Gold Rush by visiting towns like Skagway or Nome. Kids can enjoy historic reenactments, gold panning, and learning about the frontier spirit of Alaska's past. It's an engaging way to blend history with adventure.

6. Anchorage Children's Museum

For younger children, the Anchorage Children's Museum offers a world of exploration and play. Interactive exhibits encourage creativity and curiosity, making it an ideal spot for families with toddlers and young kids.

7. Dog Sledding Adventures

Alaska's state sport, dog sledding, is a thrilling experience for kids. Many tour operators offer family-friendly dog sledding trips where children can meet the sled dogs, learn about mushing, and even go for a ride.

8. Easy Hiking Trails

Alaska boasts numerous family-friendly hiking trails suitable for all ages. Consider trails like Winner Creek Trail or Thunderbird Falls Trail, which offer short, scenic walks through beautiful Alaskan landscapes.

Alaska's family-friendly activities and attractions are as diverse as the state's natural beauty. Whether your kids are wildlife enthusiasts, history buffs, or just looking for some good old-fashioned fun, Alaska has something to offer every family. Enjoy your journey through this incredible land with your loved ones!

15. Dining with Children: Family Restaurants

Exploring Alaska with your family can be an unforgettable adventure, but when it comes to dining with children in tow, it's important to find family-friendly restaurants that cater to both kids and adults. Alaska offers a variety of dining options that are perfect for families. Here, we'll guide you through some fantastic family restaurants and provide suggestions to make your dining experiences enjoyable for everyone.

1. Moose's Tooth Pub & Pizzeria, Anchorage

Why Visit: Moose's Tooth is an Anchorage institution known for its delicious pizzas, craft beers, and family-friendly atmosphere. They offer a wide range of toppings to satisfy even the pickiest eaters.

Family Tip: Try their "Totchos" – a fun twist on nachos with tater tots instead of chips. They also have a play area to keep kids entertained.

2. The Saltry Restaurant, Halibut Cove

Why Visit: Located across the bay from Homer, this charming restaurant offers stunning waterfront views and a menu featuring fresh Alaskan seafood.

Family Tip: Opt for lunch to enjoy a more relaxed atmosphere, and don't miss their famous clam chowder or fish and chips.

3. Snow City Cafe, Anchorage

Why Visit: Snow City Cafe is known for its hearty breakfast and brunch options, including mouth watering pancakes and omelets.

Family Tip: Arrive early on weekends as it's a popular spot. They offer a kids' menu and are accommodating to dietary restrictions.

4. Tracy's King Crab Shack, Juneau

Why Visit: Tracy's is a must for seafood-loving families. Feast on king crab legs, crab bisque, and other Alaskan seafood delights.

Family Tip: Share a "Crab Bucket" with the family and take in the picturesque views of Juneau's waterfront.

5. Two Sisters Bakery, Homer

Why Visit: This bakery is famous for its homemade pastries and sandwiches, making it an ideal spot for a quick and delicious family meal.

Family Tip: Grab a picnic-style lunch and head to Homer's scenic Spit for a family-friendly outing.

6. Pioneer Bar & Liquor Store, Nome

Why Visit: While not your typical family restaurant, the Pioneer Bar offers a unique experience in Nome with its rustic decor and famous reindeer hot dogs.

Family Tip: Try the reindeer hot dogs, and the kids might enjoy the quirky ambiance.

7. Beartooth Grill, Anchorage

Why Visit: Beartooth Grill combines American classics and Alaskan flavors. Their extensive menu has something for everyone.

Family Tip: Their mac 'n' cheese is a hit with kids. Enjoy a casual family dinner with Alaskan-style comfort food.

8. Gold Rush Grill, Fairbanks

Why Visit: Located in the heart of Fairbanks, this family-friendly spot offers Alaskan fare, including reindeer sausage, in a cozy setting.

Family Tip: Savor the flavors of Alaska and introduce your kids to local cuisine with reindeer sausage sliders.

When dining with children in Alaska, consider making reservations if possible, especially during peak tourist seasons. Many family restaurants in Alaska embrace the state's casual, welcoming atmosphere, making it easier for families to enjoy their meals together while savoring the local flavors.

16. Tips for Smooth Family Travel

Traveling to Alaska with your family can be an unforgettable adventure, offering a unique opportunity to bond while exploring the stunning landscapes and diverse wildlife of the Last Frontier. To ensure a smooth and enjoyable trip, here are some valuable tips for family travel in Alaska:

1. Plan Ahead: Start by researching and planning your trip well in advance. Consider the interests

and needs of each family member and create an itinerary that accommodates everyone's preferences.

2. Dress in Layers: Alaska's weather can be unpredictable. Pack clothing that can be layered for warmth, including waterproof jackets and sturdy hiking boots. Don't forget hats, gloves, and sunscreen for sun protection.

3. Kid-Friendly Activities: Alaska offers a wide range of family-friendly activities. Consider options like wildlife cruises, easy hikes, and visits to interactive museums and wildlife rehabilitation centers to keep children engaged.

4. Safety First: Teach your children about wildlife safety and the importance of respecting nature. Keep a safe distance from wild animals, and store food securely to avoid attracting them to your campsite or picnic area.

5. Wildlife Viewing: Alaska's wildlife is a highlight of any trip. Bring binoculars and a camera with a zoom lens to capture those special moments. Be patient and observant, as wildlife sightings can be unpredictable.

6. Snacks and Supplies: Stock up on snacks, water, and other essentials before heading out on day trips or hikes, as some remote areas may not have easy access to supplies.

7. Educational Opportunities: Take advantage of the educational opportunities Alaska offers. Learn about the local cultures, flora, and fauna. Engage your children in the natural world around them to create a deeper connection with the environment.

8. Flexibility: Be flexible with your schedule. Weather conditions may change plans, so have backup activities in mind. Embrace the spontaneity of your journey.

9. Accommodation: Choose family-friendly accommodations with amenities such as kitchenettes and laundry facilities. These can make your stay more comfortable and convenient.

10. Technology Breaks: Encourage your family to disconnect from screens and immerse themselves in the natural beauty of Alaska. Limit screen time to create a more enriching experience.

11. Travel Games: Bring travel-friendly board games, puzzles, or card games to keep your family entertained during downtime.

12. Responsible Travel: Emphasize the importance of responsible tourism and Leave No Trace principles. Teach your children to leave the environment as beautiful as they found it.

13. Keep Everyone Informed: Discuss the day's plans with your family each morning and ensure that everyone knows what to expect. This helps avoid surprises and keeps everyone on the same page.

14. Travel Insurance: Consider purchasing travel insurance to cover unexpected events or emergencies during your trip.

15. Capture Memories: Encourage your children to keep a travel journal or diary to document their experiences and create lasting memories.

Family travel in Alaska can be an incredible bonding experience, offering a chance to explore the wilderness, witness breathtaking landscapes, and learn about the unique cultures of the region. With careful planning and these tips in mind, you can ensure a smooth and enjoyable adventure for the whole family.

Chapter 4: Romantic Getaways for Couples

17. Romance in the Wilderness: An Alaska Experience

Alaska, with its rugged landscapes and untamed wilderness, offers couples a unique opportunity to kindle romance in the heart of nature. Whether you're celebrating a honeymoon, anniversary, or simply seeking a romantic escape, the Last Frontier has something special to offer. Here's a glimpse into the enchanting world of romance that Alaska has in store for couples.

1. Cozy Cabins and Romantic Lodges

Imagine snuggling up with your loved one in a charming, secluded cabin nestled deep in the Alaskan wilderness. Many lodges and resorts in Alaska cater specifically to couples, offering private cabins with breathtaking views of pristine lakes, snow-capped mountains, or the Northern Lights. The cozy ambiance, crackling fireplaces, and often, outdoor hot tubs provide the perfect setting for a romantic getaway.

2. Couples' Adventure Activities

For the adventurous couple, Alaska presents a plethora of thrilling experiences to share. Embark on a glacier helicopter tour and land on a secluded icefield for an exhilarating and intimate moment. Or opt for a scenic floatplane ride that takes you over Alaska's magnificent landscapes. Hiking together through lush forests or kayaking along crystal-clear waters can also create lasting memories.

3. Romantic Dining Spots

Alaska's culinary scene is as diverse as its terrain. Enjoy candlelit dinners at restaurants that offer fresh Alaskan seafood, wild game, and locally-sourced ingredients. Many establishments boast panoramic views, allowing you to savor a gourmet meal while gazing at the stunning surroundings.

4. Aurora Borealis Magic

If your visit coincides with the winter season, you might be lucky enough to witness the magic of the Northern Lights. Alaska is one of the best places on Earth to view this natural wonder. Snuggle together under a blanket as you watch the dancing lights paint the night sky with vibrant colors. It's a celestial spectacle that will leave you both in awe.

5. Secluded Beach Walks

Alaska's coastline is adorned with hidden coves and pristine beaches. Take a hand-in-hand stroll along the shore, listening to the soothing sounds of the waves crashing and watching as eagles soar overhead. It's a serene and romantic escape from the hustle and bustle of everyday life.

6. Glamping under the Stars

For a unique romantic experience, consider glamping (luxury camping) under the Alaskan stars. These accommodations offer all the comforts of a hotel room while allowing you to be surrounded by nature. Fall asleep to the sounds of nature and wake up to the calls of birds.

In Alaska, romance is not just about dinner and flowers; it's about connecting with nature and each other in a way that few places on Earth can provide. Whether you're cuddled up in a cabin, exploring the wilderness hand in hand, or watching the Northern Lights, Alaska's wilderness is the ultimate backdrop for a truly unforgettable romantic experience.

18. Cozy Cabins and Romantic Lodges

One of the most enchanting aspects of an Alaskan adventure is the opportunity to embrace the wilderness while still indulging in luxurious comfort. Alaska boasts a wealth of cozy cabins and romantic lodges that provide the perfect setting for couples seeking an intimate escape into the heart of nature. Whether you're nestled beside a pristine lake, perched on a mountainside, or hidden away in the remote wilderness, these accommodations offer an unparalleled romantic experience.

1. Secluded Cabins by the Lakeside

Imagine waking up to the gentle lapping of water against the shore, with the soft, amber hues of a sunrise painting the sky. Alaska is dotted with secluded cabins that offer this very experience. Nestled amidst lush forests and alongside serene lakes, these cabins provide couples with the ultimate privacy and tranquility. Spend your days kayaking, fishing, or simply lounging on the porch, taking in the breathtaking views of snow-capped peaks reflected in the crystal-clear waters.

2. Wilderness Retreats

For couples seeking a deeper connection with nature, consider booking a stay in a remote wilderness lodge. These lodges are often accessible only by plane or boat, ensuring an exclusive escape from the modern world. While you're far from the hustle and bustle of city life, these lodges provide cozy accommodations, gourmet dining, and an array of outdoor activities, from hiking and wildlife viewing to stargazing by the campfire.

3. Cabins with a View

Alaska's dramatic landscapes are meant to be shared, and there are cabins perched on cliffs and mountainsides that offer breathtaking panoramic views. These cabins often feature large windows and outdoor decks where you can enjoy a glass of wine while watching the sun dip below the horizon. The combination of cozy interiors and sweeping vistas creates an ambiance that's perfect for romance.

4. Hot Tubs and Northern Lights

For the ultimate romantic experience, consider staying in a cabin or lodge that offers private outdoor hot tubs. There's nothing quite like soaking in warm, bubbling water while the northern lights dance across the night sky above you. This natural light show is a spectacle that will leave you both awe-inspired and filled with wonder.

5. Rustic Elegance

While many cabins and lodges in Alaska embrace a rustic aesthetic, they are far from lacking in comfort and luxury. Expect plush bedding, cozy fireplaces, and gourmet dining options. The combination of wilderness surroundings and top-notch amenities ensures that your romantic getaway is both unforgettable and comfortable.

Alaska's cozy cabins and romantic lodges offer an escape into the untamed beauty of the Last Frontier without sacrificing the comforts and intimacy you desire. Whether you're celebrating a special occasion or simply seeking quality time together, these accommodations provide the perfect backdrop for a romantic retreat in one of the most captivating natural landscapes on Earth.

19. Couples' Adventure Activities

Alaska, with its breathtaking landscapes and diverse wilderness, offers a paradise for couples seeking adventure and romance in equal measure. Whether you're looking for heart-pounding excitement or quiet moments in nature, the Last Frontier has something to offer every couple. Here are some of the most memorable adventure activities for couples in Alaska:

1. Helicopter Tours: Soar high above Alaska's stunning terrain in a private helicopter tour. Witness glaciers, rugged mountains, and pristine lakes from a vantage point that few get to experience. Many tours even offer glacier landings, where you can step out onto the ice for a truly surreal moment.

2. Dog Sledding: Embrace the spirit of the Iditarod by mushing your own team of huskies through Alaska's wilderness. Share the thrill of gliding across the snow-covered landscapes while bonding with these remarkable canine companions.

3. Whale Watching: Witness the awe-inspiring sight of majestic humpback whales breaching the surface. Take a romantic cruise together to spot these gentle giants along with orcas, gray whales, and other marine life in the pristine waters off Alaska's coast.

4. Hiking and Backcountry Camping: For couples who love the great outdoors, Alaska offers an extensive network of hiking trails through its

national parks and forests. Embark on a multi-day trek, set up camp beneath the starry sky, and savor the tranquility of the wilderness together.

5. Hot Springs Retreats: Find relaxation and romance in Alaska's natural hot springs. There are several remote hot spring locations where you can unwind in warm mineral-rich waters surrounded by snow-capped mountains and the serenity of nature.

6. Sea Kayaking: Explore Alaska's coastal wonders by paddling together in a sea kayak. Glide past towering icebergs, watch sea otters play, and admire the beauty of the coastline. Many tours offer guided excursions suitable for all skill levels.

7. Zip Lining: Experience an adrenaline rush by zip-lining through the treetops of Alaska's lush forests. It's a thrilling way to bond as you conquer challenges and take in the incredible scenery.

8. Northern Lights Viewing: Witnessing the Northern Lights, or Aurora Borealis, is a magical experience for any couple. Head to northern Alaska during the winter months to witness the dancing lights in the night sky together.

9. Wildlife Safaris: Share the excitement of wildlife encounters on guided safaris. Spot grizzly bears, moose, eagles, and more in their natural habitats. Many tour operators offer photography-focused tours for those seeking to capture these moments forever.

10. Rock Climbing and Ice Climbing: For adventurous couples with a passion for climbing, Alaska offers world-class rock and ice climbing opportunities. Guided excursions are available for all skill levels, providing thrilling challenges and breathtaking views.

Whether you're seeking heart-pounding adventure or tranquil moments in nature, Alaska's diverse range of activities ensures that couples can create lasting memories together in this awe-inspiring wilderness. From helicopter rides over glaciers to intimate moments beneath the Northern Lights, Alaska offers a unique and unforgettable experience for couples seeking adventure and connection in the great outdoors.

20. Romantic Dining Spots

Alaska's pristine wilderness and stunning landscapes provide the perfect backdrop for romantic moments, and what better way to complement those moments than with a memorable dining experience? Whether you're celebrating an anniversary, honeymoon, or just looking to enjoy a special meal together, Alaska offers a variety of romantic dining spots that will leave you and your loved one with cherished memories.

1. The Crow's Nest - Anchorage:
Located atop the Captain Cook Hotel in downtown Anchorage, The Crow's Nest is renowned for its panoramic views of the city, Cook Inlet, and the surrounding mountains. This upscale restaurant offers a menu featuring fresh Alaskan seafood, delectable steaks, and an extensive wine list. Reserve a window table for a breathtaking sunset dinner.

2. Seven Glaciers - Girdwood:
Nestled in the Alyeska Resort, Seven Glaciers is accessed via an aerial tramway, setting the stage for a truly unique dining experience. With its glacier and mountain views, this restaurant specializes in modern Alaskan cuisine, including dishes prepared with locally sourced ingredients.

3. The Saltry Restaurant - Halibut Cove:

For an intimate and secluded dining experience, venture to The Saltry Restaurant on Ismailof Island in Halibut Cove. Accessible only by boat, this charming eatery is surrounded by the natural beauty of Kachemak Bay State Park. Enjoy fresh seafood, garden-grown produce, and a serene atmosphere.

4. Simon & Seaforts - Anchorage:
A classic choice for a romantic dinner in Anchorage, Simon & Seaforts offers a blend of Alaskan and Pacific Rim flavors. Their waterfront location provides a view of the Cook Inlet and the Chugach Mountains. Sunset dining on the deck is particularly romantic.

5. The Pump House - Fairbanks:
Situated along the Chena River in Fairbanks, The Pump House combines history with elegance. This rustic yet refined restaurant is known for its Alaskan game dishes, fresh seafood, and extensive wine selection. Enjoy your meal on the outdoor deck overlooking the river.

6. Orso - Anchorage:
Orso offers a warm and inviting ambiance with a menu that focuses on contemporary Italian cuisine with an Alaskan twist. It's an excellent choice for

couples seeking a cozy and romantic dinner in downtown Anchorage.

7. The Inn at Tern Lake - Moose Pass:
For an enchanting dining experience on the Kenai Peninsula, visit The Inn at Tern Lake. This charming inn and restaurant offer an intimate setting with views of Tern Lake and the surrounding mountains. The menu features gourmet cuisine with a seasonal flair.

Remember to make reservations in advance, especially during the busy tourist season, to secure your table at these romantic dining spots. Whether you're sharing a candlelit dinner overlooking a glacier or enjoying fresh seafood by the water's edge, Alaska's romantic dining venues will help you create unforgettable moments with your loved one.

21. Tips for a Memorable Couple's Retreat

Alaska's rugged beauty and serene landscapes provide the perfect backdrop for a romantic retreat. Whether you're celebrating an anniversary, honeymoon, or simply seeking quality time together, Alaska offers a unique and unforgettable experience for couples. Here are some tips to make your couple's retreat in Alaska truly memorable:

1. Choose the Right Season:
   - Alaska's seasons vary dramatically. Consider what activities and weather you prefer. Summer offers extended daylight and mild temperatures, while winter provides a magical, snow-covered landscape. Spring and fall offer unique opportunities for fewer crowds.

2. Cozy Accommodations:
   - Opt for cozy lodges, cabins, or romantic bed-and-breakfasts. Many accommodations feature private hot tubs, fireplaces, and stunning views, creating an intimate atmosphere.

3. Scenic Drives:
   - Plan scenic road trips along Alaska's picturesque highways like the Seward Highway, the Denali Highway, or the Dalton Highway. These routes offer breathtaking vistas, wildlife sightings, and plenty of spots for picnics and photos.

4. Wildlife Encounters:
   - Go on a wildlife watching adventure together. Alaska is home to bears, moose, whales, and eagles. Consider a guided tour for safe and informative encounters.

5. Adventure Activities:

- Bond over thrilling activities like hiking, kayaking, or zip-lining. Share the excitement of exploring Alaska's wilderness and conquering new challenges together.

6. Northern Lights Viewing:
   - If visiting during the winter months, witnessing the Northern Lights (Aurora Borealis) is a must. Head to remote areas with minimal light pollution for the best viewing experience.

7. Romantic Dining:
   - Alaska boasts exquisite seafood and unique dining experiences. Book a romantic dinner at a waterfront restaurant or savor fresh-caught salmon in a cozy lodge setting.

8. Hot Springs Retreat:
   - Unwind together at one of Alaska's natural hot springs. Soaking in geothermal pools surrounded by nature is both relaxing and romantic.

9. Stargazing:
   - Alaska's vast wilderness provides excellent stargazing opportunities. Bring a telescope or simply lay out under the night sky to admire the constellations.

10. Plan Alone Time:
   - Allocate moments for just the two of you. Whether it's a secluded picnic, a private boat tour, or a quiet moment by the campfire, cherish your alone time in this beautiful setting.

11. Capture the Moments:
   - Don't forget to document your trip with photos and journaling. These memories will be cherished for years to come.

12. Disconnect and Reconnect:
   - Consider limiting screen time and focusing on each other and the natural surroundings. Disconnecting from the digital world can enhance your connection as a couple.

13. Respect the Environment:
   - Practice responsible tourism by following Leave No Trace principles. Preserve Alaska's pristine wilderness for future generations to enjoy.

A couple's retreat in Alaska promises adventure, romance, and unforgettable moments. With the right planning and a spirit of adventure, you can create lasting memories in this wild and beautiful destination.

Chapter 5: Exploring Alaska's Regions

22. Anchorage and the Southcentral Region

Nestled between the Chugach Mountains and the shores of Cook Inlet, Anchorage serves as the perfect introduction to the remarkable beauty of Southcentral Alaska. As the state's largest city, Anchorage is often regarded as the gateway to the wild and rugged landscapes that define Alaska's essence.

Anchorage Highlights:
  - Anchorage Downtown: Start your exploration in the heart of the city, where you'll find a vibrant downtown district with an array of shops, restaurants, and cultural attractions.
  - Alaska Native Heritage Center: Discover the rich cultural heritage of Alaska's indigenous peoples through engaging exhibits and live demonstrations.
  - Anchorage Museum: Immerse yourself in the art, history, and science of Alaska with interactive exhibits and fascinating displays.
  - Tony Knowles Coastal Trail: This scenic 11-mile trail offers breathtaking views of the surrounding mountains and the opportunity to spot wildlife along the coastal shoreline.
  - Alaska Wildlife Conservation Center: Just a short drive from Anchorage, this center allows you to

observe native Alaskan wildlife, including bears, moose, and eagles.

Exploring the Southcentral Region: Wilderness at Your Doorstep

Beyond Anchorage lies the vast Southcentral Region, a diverse landscape that combines urban conveniences with unparalleled natural beauty.

Kenai Peninsula:
  - Kenai Fjords National Park: Take a boat tour to witness towering glaciers calving into the ocean and marvel at the marine wildlife, including whales, seals, and puffins.
  - Homer: Known as the "Halibut Fishing Capital of the World," this charming town offers excellent fishing, art galleries, and stunning views of Kachemak Bay.

Matanuska-Susitna Valley:
  - Matanuska Glacier: Explore this accessible glacier, either on foot or with a guided ice trek, for an up-close encounter with the power of nature.
  - Talkeetna: A quaint town known for its vibrant arts scene and as a base for climbers attempting Denali, North America's highest peak.

Prince William Sound:
 - Valdez: Discover this coastal town surrounded by stunning glaciers and embark on a kayak adventure to explore serene fjords and spot sea otters and bald eagles.

Practical Tips:
- Southcentral Alaska's weather can be unpredictable, so pack layers and rain gear.
- Consider a rental car for exploring the region, as many attractions are spread out.
- Local cuisine includes fresh seafood, particularly salmon and halibut; be sure to savor these delicacies during your visit.

From the vibrant streets of Anchorage to the untamed wilderness of the Southcentral Region, this part of Alaska offers a seamless blend of urban comforts and unparalleled natural beauty, making it a must-visit destination for any traveler seeking the essence of the Last Frontier.

23. Denali National Park and the Interior

One of the crown jewels of an Alaskan adventure is undoubtedly Denali National Park and the surrounding Interior region. This pristine wilderness area, located in the heart of Alaska, offers travelers a chance to immerse themselves in the untamed beauty of the Last Frontier. Whether you're a solo traveler, a family with kids, or a couple seeking a romantic escape, Denali and the Interior have something awe-inspiring for everyone.

Getting There:
- Denali National Park is accessible by road, primarily through the George Parks Highway (Route 3) that connects Anchorage to Fairbanks.
- Visitors can also opt for train journeys, offering breathtaking views of the landscape.

Spectacular Denali National Park:
- The centerpiece of the Interior, Denali National Park is renowned for its namesake, Denali, North America's tallest peak.
- Exploring the park is a must, with various options such as shuttle buses, guided tours, or self-driving (limited access).
- Wildlife enthusiasts can spot grizzly bears, moose, wolves, and more against the backdrop of stunning mountain scenery.

Activities and Adventures:
- Hiking: Denali offers a range of trails, from easy walks to challenging backcountry hikes.
- Wildlife Viewing: The park is a haven for wildlife, and the open tundra makes spotting animals easier.

- Flightseeing: Take to the skies for jaw-dropping aerial views of Denali and the park's rugged terrain.
- Rafting: The Nenana River provides thrilling whitewater rafting opportunities.

Family-Friendly Fun:
- Denali welcomes families with special Junior Ranger programs and kid-friendly hikes.
- Campgrounds offer a chance for kids to connect with nature like never before.
- Wildlife tours are perfect for young adventurers, allowing them to learn about Alaskan animals up close.

Romantic Escapes:
- Cozy lodges and cabins around the park provide a romantic retreat.
- Stargazing: The Interior's low light pollution offers an unforgettable celestial experience.
- Private tours can be arranged for couples seeking solitude amidst breathtaking landscapes.

Local Culture and Heritage:
- Visit the Alaska Native Heritage Center to learn about indigenous cultures.
- Attend cultural events and festivals to immerse yourself in local traditions.

Practical Tips:
- Weather can be unpredictable, so pack layers and be prepared for changing conditions.
- Make advance reservations for accommodations, especially during the peak summer season.
- Practice Leave No Trace principles to preserve the wilderness.

Exploring Denali National Park and the Interior is a profound and humbling experience. It's a place where the majesty of nature takes center stage, and every traveler, whether solo, with family, or as a couple, can create lasting memories amidst Alaska's untamed beauty. From the rugged mountains to the endless wilderness, this region embodies the spirit of adventure that Alaska is known for.

24. The Alaska Panhandle: Southeastern Adventures

The Alaska Panhandle, often referred to as Southeast Alaska, is a region unlike any other in the state. It's a place where towering fjords, lush rainforests, and pristine waterways converge to create a breathtaking natural wonderland. This area, which stretches along the southeastern coast of Alaska, offers travelers a unique blend of outdoor adventures, cultural richness, and abundant wildlife.

Getting to The Alaska Panhandle

The primary gateway to the Alaska Panhandle is via air or sea. Most visitors arrive by flying into Juneau, the state's capital, which is only accessible by air or water due to its isolation. Alternatively, cruise ships frequently make stops in popular ports like Juneau, Ketchikan, and Sitka, providing passengers with a scenic introduction to the region.

Exploring Juneau: Alaska's Capital

Juneau, the heart of the Alaska Panhandle, boasts a captivating blend of history and natural beauty. Highlights in and around the city include:

1. Mendenhall Glacier: Witness the awe-inspiring beauty of this glacier, located just 13 miles from downtown Juneau. Hiking trails, wildlife viewing, and visitor centers provide various ways to experience its grandeur.

2. Tracy Arm Fjord: Embark on a boat tour to Tracy Arm, a glacier-carved fjord known for its towering ice formations, dramatic cliffs, and abundant wildlife.

3. Historic Downtown: Stroll through Juneau's charming downtown, dotted with historic buildings, art galleries, and locally-owned shops.

Ketchikan: The Salmon Capital of the World

Ketchikan, often dubbed the Salmon Capital of the World, offers a unique blend of Native culture and outdoor activities:

1. Totem Heritage Center: Explore the rich Native American heritage of the Tlingit, Haida, and Tsimshian peoples through an impressive collection of totem poles and artifacts.

2. Creek Street: Wander along this historic boardwalk lined with quirky shops, galleries, and a dose of Ketchikan's colorful history.

3. Salmon Fishing: Join a fishing expedition to experience the thrill of reeling in salmon from the abundant waters surrounding Ketchikan.

Sitka: Where History and Nature Converge

Sitka, with its Russian history and stunning natural surroundings, offers a unique Alaskan experience:

1. Sitka National Historical Park: Immerse yourself in Alaskan history at this park, home to a collection of totem poles and a visitor center offering cultural insights.

2. Sea Kayaking: Paddle through Sitka's tranquil bays and inlets, observing wildlife such as sea otters, whales, and bald eagles.

3. Fortress of the Bear: Witness rescued bears in a natural rainforest setting, learning about bear conservation efforts.

Outdoor Adventures in the Alaska Panhandle

Southeast Alaska is an outdoor enthusiast's paradise, offering activities such as:

1. Hiking: Explore rainforest trails, like the Tongass National Forest, offering hiking opportunities for all skill levels.

2. Wildlife Cruises: Take boat excursions to observe humpback whales, orca whales, sea lions, and puffins in their natural habitat.

3. Sea Kayaking: Paddle through serene waterways, camping on remote islands for a true wilderness experience.

The Alaska Panhandle, with its captivating blend of natural wonders, cultural richness, and outdoor adventures, is a must-visit destination for travelers seeking an unforgettable Alaskan experience. Whether you arrive by cruise ship or by air, the beauty and diversity of this region will leave you with lasting memories of your Southeastern Alaska adventure.

25. *Fairbanks and the Interior North*

The Interior North of Alaska is a region of stark beauty and unique experiences, with Fairbanks at its heart. Known for its rich history, diverse culture, and unparalleled natural wonders, this part of the Last Frontier promises an adventure like no other.

Fairbanks: The Golden Heart City

Fairbanks, often referred to as the "Golden Heart City," is the largest city in the Interior North and serves as the gateway to the Arctic. Here, you'll find a blend of modern amenities and a deep connection to the region's history and natural surroundings.

1. Pioneer Park: Begin your journey by exploring Pioneer Park, a living museum that captures the essence of Fairbanks' early days. Visit the Alaska Museum to learn about the state's history and indigenous cultures.

2. Riverboat Discovery: Take a leisurely cruise on the Riverboat Discovery, a replica steamboat that navigates the Chena and Tanana Rivers. You'll witness a working sled dog kennel and experience a firsthand glimpse of Alaska's unique way of life.

3. Aurora Borealis Viewing: Fairbanks is one of the best places on Earth to witness the mesmerizing Northern Lights. Plan your visit during the winter months for the best chance to see this natural wonder. Various tours and lodges offer prime viewing locations.

4. Chena Hot Springs: Soak in the rejuvenating waters of Chena Hot Springs, set against a backdrop of snowy wilderness. This geothermal oasis is perfect for unwinding after a day of exploration.

Venturing Further into the Interior North

Beyond Fairbanks, the Interior North offers a diverse range of attractions and activities:

5. Denali National Park: Head south to Denali National Park and Preserve, home to North America's tallest peak, Denali (formerly Mount McKinley). Explore the park's pristine wilderness, go hiking, or embark on a wildlife tour to spot grizzly bears, moose, and caribou.

6. Alaska's Gold Rush History: The Interior North played a pivotal role in the Klondike Gold Rush. Visit the historic town of Nome, where you can pan for gold and explore gold rush relics.

7. Hot Springs and Geothermal Pools: Besides Chena Hot Springs, you can find other natural hot springs and geothermal pools scattered throughout the region. They provide a warm and soothing respite in the midst of the Alaskan wilderness.

8. Arctic Circle Adventures: For the truly adventurous, consider a journey to the Arctic Circle. Tours from Fairbanks will take you across the rugged Dalton Highway, where you'll cross the Arctic Circle and witness the dramatic landscapes of the Arctic tundra.

9. Cultural Experiences: Immerse yourself in the rich cultural heritage of Alaska's indigenous peoples. Visit places like the Morris Thompson Cultural and Visitors Center in Fairbanks to learn about Athabascan traditions and art.

Exploring Fairbanks and the Interior North of Alaska offers a unique blend of history, culture, and natural wonders. Whether you're gazing at the Northern Lights in Fairbanks, hiking in Denali National Park, or panning for gold, this region will leave you with unforgettable memories of the Last Frontier.

26. Discovering the Far North: The Arctic Region

The Arctic region of Alaska is a land of breathtaking extremes, a place where the rugged beauty of the wilderness meets the stark reality of a polar climate. This remote and unique corner of the state offers intrepid travelers a chance to experience the true essence of Alaska. Here, in this part, we'll delve into what makes exploring the Arctic region an unforgettable adventure.

Getting There
The journey to the Arctic region is an adventure in itself. Most travelers fly into Fairbanks, the gateway

to the Arctic, and from there, they can access the far north by road, air, or even river travel. The Dalton Highway, also known as the "Haul Road," is a famous route that leads north through some of the most remote and pristine wilderness in North America.

The Unique Landscape
As you venture further north, you'll witness a dramatic shift in the landscape. The boreal forests give way to tundra, and eventually, you'll find yourself in the land of the midnight sun, where the Arctic Circle marks the boundary of constant daylight during the summer months. The region's rivers and lakes are often frozen for much of the year, providing opportunities for ice fishing and snowmobiling in the winter.

Wildlife Encounters
The Arctic region is a haven for wildlife enthusiasts. Here, you can witness iconic Arctic species such as polar bears, caribou, muskoxen, and Arctic foxes in their natural habitats. Birdwatchers will be delighted by the countless migratory birds that flock to the Arctic during the summer.

Cultural Immersion

One of the most rewarding aspects of exploring the Arctic is the chance to engage with the indigenous communities that have called this harsh environment home for centuries. Learning about the traditional Inupiaq and Yupik cultures provides a deep insight into the resilience and resourcefulness required to survive in such extreme conditions.

Outdoor Adventures
The Arctic region offers a wide range of outdoor activities for adventurers of all levels. From hiking and backpacking in the Brooks Range to kayaking along the Arctic coastline, there are plenty of ways to immerse yourself in the pristine wilderness. Winter activities like dog sledding and snowshoeing under the Northern Lights are a once-in-a-lifetime experience.

When to Go
The Arctic region's climate is extreme, with very cold winters and short, mild summers. Most travelers opt to visit during the summer months, from late June to early September when the days are long and the temperatures are relatively mild.

Practical Tips

Visiting the Arctic region requires careful planning. It's essential to be well-prepared for the harsh conditions, including cold weather gear and reliable transportation. Additionally, due to the remoteness, it's wise to have contingency plans in place in case of unexpected challenges.

Exploring the Arctic region in Alaska is an adventure like no other. It's a place where the untamed wilderness and the spirit of exploration converge. Whether you're a wildlife enthusiast, a cultural explorer, or simply seeking the thrill of the unknown, the Arctic region offers an unparalleled journey into the heart of Alaska's wilderness.

27. Western Alaska: Off-the-Beaten-Path Treasures

Western Alaska is a vast and remote region that beckons travelers seeking an authentic and off-the-beaten-path Alaskan experience. This untamed wilderness is characterized by rugged landscapes, pristine waters, and a rich indigenous heritage. Here, you'll discover a unique blend of natural beauty and cultural diversity that defines this part of the Last Frontier.

1. The Aleutian Islands

The Aleutian Islands stretch like a chain of jewels from the Alaska Peninsula into the Bering Sea. These volcanic islands are a paradise for nature enthusiasts and history buffs alike. Explore remote villages, where the Aleut people have thrived for thousands of years. Witness the astounding birdlife, including puffins and bald eagles, and visit the haunting World War II relics that dot the landscape.

2. Nome and the Gold Rush Legacy
Nome, a small town with a big history, is synonymous with the Alaskan Gold Rush of the late 19th century. Today, visitors can still try their hand at gold panning and hear tales of the daring prospectors who once flocked here. Nome is also renowned for its bird migration, making it a birdwatcher's paradise during the summer months.

3. The Yukon River and its Tributaries
Flowing through the heart of Western Alaska, the Yukon River and its tributaries offer a unique opportunity for river-based adventures. Take a riverboat cruise to experience the remote villages and historic sites along its banks. Or, for the more adventurous, embark on a kayak or canoe expedition to immerse yourself in the pristine wilderness.

4. Bethel and Native Alaskan Cultures
Bethel, the largest community in the Yukon-Kuskokwim Delta, serves as a gateway to the rich cultures of the Yup'ik and Cup'ik Eskimo peoples. Explore local art galleries, try traditional foods, and engage in cultural activities that provide insight into the indigenous way of life. Don't miss the annual Camai Dance Festival, a celebration of dance, music, and storytelling.

5. Lake Clark National Park and Preserve
This lesser-known gem offers a wilderness experience like no other. Accessible only by small aircraft or boat, Lake Clark National Park and Preserve boasts stunning landscapes, including glaciers, volcanoes, and pristine lakes. Hike along scenic trails, watch for bears and other wildlife, and camp beneath the star-studded Alaskan sky.

6. Togiak National Wildlife Refuge
Togiak National Wildlife Refuge is a remote and wild expanse of land and water. It's a prime destination for those seeking solitude and natural beauty. Fishing enthusiasts flock here for world-class salmon and trout fishing. Birdwatchers can spot a wide array of migratory birds, and wildlife photographers will find endless

opportunities to capture the essence of Alaska's untamed wilderness.

7. The Spirit of Western Alaska
Exploring Western Alaska is about connecting with the spirit of the land and its people. Be prepared for rustic accommodations, limited amenities, and the challenge of traveling in a remote environment. But the rewards are immeasurable: the chance to witness the unspoiled beauty of Alaska, to meet indigenous communities preserving their traditions, and to experience a sense of adventure that can only be found off the beaten path.

When visiting Western Alaska, remember to plan ahead, respect the environment, and embrace the unique opportunity to explore a part of Alaska that remains a well-guarded secret among intrepid travelers.

Chapter 6: Outdoor Adventures

28. Hiking and Trekking in Alaska's Wilderness

Alaska's rugged and untamed wilderness offers some of the most awe-inspiring hiking and trekking opportunities in the world. From towering mountain ranges to vast tundra expanses, the state beckons outdoor enthusiasts to explore its remote and pristine landscapes. Whether you're a seasoned hiker or a beginner looking for an adventure, Alaska has something to offer everyone.

1. Choosing Your Trail

Alaska boasts an extensive network of hiking trails, each with its unique charm. Here are some must-visit destinations for hikers and trekkers:

- Denali National Park: Home to North America's highest peak, Denali, this park offers a range of hiking trails, from easy strolls to challenging multi-day treks.

- Chugach State Park: Located near Anchorage, this park features an array of trails, including the popular Crow Pass Trail, known for its breathtaking scenery.

- Kenai Peninsula: Explore the rugged beauty of the Kenai Peninsula, with trails like the Harding Icefield Trail leading to stunning glacier views.

- Wrangell-St. Elias National Park: The largest national park in the U.S. offers remote and challenging treks amid towering peaks.

2. Preparation and Safety

Before embarking on your hiking adventure, consider the following:

- Weather: Alaska's weather can be unpredictable. Dress in layers, and always carry rain gear and warm clothing, even in summer.

- Wildlife: Be bear aware. Learn how to use bear-resistant containers for food storage and make noise on the trail to avoid surprise encounters.

- Navigation: Carry maps, a compass, and a GPS device. Cell phone reception is often limited in remote areas.

- Permits: Some trails require permits, especially in national parks. Check the regulations and obtain necessary permits in advance.

3. Wildlife Encounters

Alaska's wilderness is teeming with wildlife, including bears, moose, eagles, and more. To make the most of your experience while staying safe:

- Keep a safe distance from all wildlife. Respect their space and do not approach or feed them.

- Make noise while hiking to alert animals to your presence.

- Familiarize yourself with bear safety protocols, including carrying bear spray and knowing how to use it.

4. Leave No Trace

Alaska's pristine wilderness is fragile. Follow Leave No Trace principles:

- Pack out everything you bring with you, including trash and waste.

- Stay on designated trails to minimize impact on vegetation.

- Camp in established campsites, and use established fire rings if fires are permitted.

5. Guided Tours and Resources

If you're new to Alaska or prefer guided experiences, consider joining a guided hiking tour. Knowledgeable guides can enhance your adventure and ensure safety.

Alaska offers a wealth of resources for hikers and trekkers, including visitor centers, ranger stations, and local outfitters. Take advantage of these resources to plan your journey and get updates on trail conditions.

In Alaska's wilderness, you'll discover a profound connection with nature and experience landscapes that will leave you in awe. Hiking and trekking in this pristine environment is an adventure you'll cherish forever, providing memories of breathtaking vistas, encounters with wildlife, and the joy of exploring one of the last frontiers on Earth.

29. Wildlife Encounters: Watching and Safety

Alaska is a wildlife enthusiast's paradise, offering some of the most breathtaking and diverse animal encounters on the planet. From grizzly bears in Denali National Park to humpback whales breaching in the icy waters of the Inside Passage, the opportunities to observe Alaska's magnificent creatures are endless. However, with great beauty comes great responsibility. Wildlife encounters in Alaska should be awe-inspiring and safe, both for you and the animals.

Watching Wildlife Responsibly

1. Respect Viewing Guidelines: Many parks and wildlife reserves have specific guidelines for observing animals. Follow them diligently, whether it's maintaining a safe distance or using binoculars to avoid disturbing nesting birds.

2. Stay Quiet and Patient: Wildlife watching often requires patience. Keep noise to a minimum, as sudden loud sounds can startle animals. Wait quietly, and you may be rewarded with a more natural and undisturbed encounter.

3. Use Binoculars and Telephoto Lenses: Instead of getting too close to animals, invest in quality binoculars or a telephoto camera lens to observe them from a safe distance.

4. Observe from Designated Viewing Areas: Many popular wildlife-watching spots have designated viewing areas or platforms. Use these areas to minimize your impact on the environment.

Safety Measures

1. Bear Safety: Alaska is bear country, and knowing how to behave around them is crucial. Carry bear spray, make noise to announce your presence on trails, and store food properly to avoid attracting bears to your campsite.

2. Moose Encounters: While moose may appear docile, they can be unpredictable. Maintain a safe distance, especially if you encounter a moose with calves. Do not approach them or attempt to feed them.

3. Marine Wildlife: When observing marine mammals like whales and seals, maintain a respectful distance and avoid approaching them with boats or kayaks too closely. Federal laws

protect marine wildlife in Alaska, so familiarize yourself with these regulations.

4. Bird Nesting Areas: If you're a birdwatcher, be aware of nesting areas during the breeding season. Keep your distance to avoid disturbing nesting birds and their chicks.

5. Weather Awareness: Alaska's weather can change rapidly, and hypothermia is a real risk. Dress in layers, carry rain gear, and be prepared for sudden temperature drops, even in summer.

6. Emergency Communication: In remote areas, it's crucial to have a reliable means of communication in case of emergencies. Consider a satellite phone or a personal locator beacon.

Remember that you are a guest in these animals' homes, and your primary goal should be to observe them without causing stress or harm. Respect for the wildlife and the environment ensures that future generations can also enjoy Alaska's incredible natural wonders. By following these guidelines, you can have memorable and safe wildlife encounters in the Last Frontier.

30. Fishing and Boating in Alaska's Waters

Alaska's pristine waters offer some of the world's most renowned fishing and boating experiences, making it a haven for anglers and adventurers alike. In this part, we dive into the thrill of fishing and boating in Alaska's vast and untamed aquatic landscapes.

Fishing Adventures

Alaska is a fisherman's paradise, boasting five species of salmon (King, Silver, Sockeye, Pink, and Chum), halibut, trout, arctic char, and more. Whether you're a seasoned angler or a novice, there's a fishing experience for everyone:

1. Salmon Fishing: Discover the best locations and seasons for salmon fishing. Learn the art of fly fishing, spin casting, and trolling while chasing these prized fish.

2. Halibut Fishing: Head to the coastal waters for a chance to catch enormous halibut. Charter boats provide all the necessary equipment and expertise.

3. Trout and Char Fishing: Explore Alaska's pristine rivers and lakes to reel in trophy-sized rainbow trout and arctic char.

4. Ice Fishing: In winter, embrace the cold and try ice fishing on frozen lakes. It's an unforgettable experience with spectacular views of snowy landscapes.

Boating Adventures

Boating is a gateway to Alaska's remote and breathtaking scenery. Whether you're a kayaker, canoeist, or prefer larger vessels, there's an adventure awaiting you:

1. Sea Kayaking: Paddle through fjords and alongside glaciers in sea kayaks. Witness calving glaciers and spot marine life up close.

2. Canoeing: Explore the tranquil rivers and lakes of Alaska by canoe. It's a serene way to connect with nature.

3. Cruise Adventures: Embark on a cruise to Alaska's Inside Passage. Witness wildlife, glaciers, and coastal towns from the comfort of a cruise ship.

4. Boat Tours: Join guided boat tours to remote areas, including wildlife sanctuaries and birdwatching hotspots.

Boating and Fishing Tips

- Gear and Equipment: Learn about the essential gear and clothing you'll need for boating and fishing in Alaska's diverse conditions.

- Safety Precautions: Understand the importance of safety measures, including life jackets, bear safety, and navigation.

- Local Regulations: Familiarize yourself with fishing regulations, bag limits, and licenses required for both residents and non-residents.

- Responsible Fishing: Emphasize responsible fishing practices to protect the delicate ecosystems and sustain the fish populations.

Whether you're casting a line into a remote river, cruising among glaciers, or exploring the intricate waterways of the Inside Passage, Alaska's waters offer an unparalleled connection with nature. This chapter equips you with the knowledge and inspiration to embark on your own aquatic adventure in the Last Frontier.

31. Winter Wonderland: Activities in the Snow

Welcome to Alaska's enchanting Winter Wonderland! While many travelers flock to the state during the warmer months, don't underestimate the magic and adventure that Alaska offers in winter. From glistening snowscapes to thrilling cold-weather activities, here's your guide to making the most of an Alaskan winter wonderland.

1. Snowshoeing and Cross-Country Skiing
Embrace the serene beauty of Alaska's snow-covered landscapes with snowshoeing and cross-country skiing. Trails abound, offering options for all skill levels. Glide silently through tranquil forests, across frozen lakes, and even catch glimpses of wildlife tracks in the snow.

2. Dog Sledding
Experience the exhilaration of dog sledding, an iconic Alaskan activity. Let a team of spirited huskies whisk you through snow-covered trails, guided by seasoned mushers. This is not just an adventure; it's a journey into the heart of Alaskan winter tradition.

3. Ice Fishing

Venture out onto frozen lakes and rivers to partake in ice fishing. Drop your line through the ice and try your luck at catching salmon, trout, or Arctic char. Local guides provide all the gear and expertise you need for a memorable day on the ice.

4. Northern Lights Viewing
Alaska is one of the best places on Earth to witness the mesmerizing Northern Lights, also known as the Aurora Borealis. Head to regions like Fairbanks or the Arctic for the highest chances of witnessing this celestial spectacle. Keep an eye on the aurora forecasts and be prepared for some late-night winter magic.

5. Winter Wildlife Tours
Winter is an excellent time for wildlife viewing in Alaska. Take a guided tour to spot magnificent creatures like moose, wolves, and bald eagles against the backdrop of a pristine snowy landscape. Bundle up, grab your camera, and set out on an unforgettable safari.

6. Ice Sculpting and Winter Festivals
Discover the artistry of ice sculpting at various winter festivals and events held throughout the state. Watch talented sculptors transform blocks of ice into intricate masterpieces. Don't miss the

chance to join in on the festivities, which often include sledding, ice skating, and local cuisine.

7. Relax in Hot Springs
Warm up in natural hot springs while surrounded by snowy panoramas. Alaska boasts numerous hot springs, such as Chena Hot Springs near Fairbanks. Soak in the soothing mineral waters, and if you're lucky, catch a glimpse of the Northern Lights while you relax.

8. Snowmobiling
For those seeking adrenaline-pumping adventures, hop on a snowmobile and explore Alaska's backcountry. With miles of groomed trails and vast expanses of untouched snow, it's an ideal way to experience the wild side of winter.

9. Winter Photography
Capture the beauty of Alaska's winter wonderland through the lens of your camera. Snow-covered mountains, frozen waterfalls, and pristine forests offer endless opportunities for breathtaking winter photography.

10. Cozy Cabins and Fireside Retreats
Wrap up your snowy adventures with a cozy cabin stay or a fireside retreat. Alaska's remote cabins

provide a rustic yet warm and inviting atmosphere, allowing you to unwind and reflect on your day's adventures.

Remember, Alaska's winter wonderland is a playground for those who appreciate the quiet majesty of snow-covered landscapes and the thrill of cold-weather activities. Whether you're an outdoor enthusiast or simply seeking a serene escape, Alaska in winter promises an unforgettable experience. So, bundle up, embrace the chill, and let Alaska's snowy charms captivate your heart.

32. *Camping and RV Travel Tips*

Camping and RV travel offer incredible opportunities to immerse yourself in Alaska's natural beauty and experience the wilderness up close. Alaska's vast landscapes, national parks, and scenic byways provide the perfect backdrop for outdoor enthusiasts. Here are some essential tips for making the most of your camping and RV adventure in Alaska:

1. Choose Your Campground Wisely:
   - Alaska offers a range of campgrounds, from remote and rustic to fully equipped.

- Research campgrounds in advance and make reservations when possible, especially during the peak summer season.

2. Be Bear Aware:
   - Alaska is bear country, so it's crucial to follow bear safety protocols.
   - Store food and trash securely, and use bear-resistant containers if available.
   - Carry bear spray and know how to use it.

3. Pack for All Seasons:
   - Alaska's weather can change rapidly, so pack layers and be prepared for rain, wind, and even snow, depending on the season and location.
   - Don't forget insect repellent for those pesky mosquitoes in summer.

4. RV Travel Tips:
   - Ensure your RV is well-maintained before your trip, as services can be limited in some areas.
   - Plan your route, considering the size of your RV and any restrictions on roads or bridges.
   - Be mindful of wildlife when driving; moose and other animals can unexpectedly appear on the road.

5. Leave No Trace:

- Follow Leave No Trace principles to minimize your impact on the environment.
- Pack out all trash, and dispose of waste in designated areas.

6. Water and Supplies:
- Carry ample water, as potable water sources can be limited in some areas.
- Stock up on supplies, including groceries and camping essentials, before heading into more remote regions.

7. Campfire Regulations:
- Check local regulations regarding campfires, as they may be restricted or prohibited in some areas.
- Bring a camp stove for cooking instead.

8. Plan for Connectivity:
- Expect limited cell phone reception in many parts of Alaska.
- Consider investing in a satellite phone or two-way communication device for emergencies.

9. Wildlife Viewing:
- Respect wildlife from a safe distance, and use binoculars or telephoto lenses for close-up views.
- Attend ranger-led programs in national parks for expert guidance on wildlife watching.

10. Permits and Regulations:
   - Research and obtain any necessary permits for camping, fishing, or hunting activities.
   - Familiarize yourself with state and federal regulations regarding outdoor activities.

11. Be Flexible:
   - Alaska's weather and road conditions can be unpredictable, so have a flexible itinerary.
   - Embrace spontaneity and seize opportunities for wildlife sightings and scenic detours.

Camping and RV travel in Alaska provide a unique chance to experience the state's untouched wilderness. By following these tips and being well-prepared, you can make the most of your outdoor adventure while respecting the natural environment and wildlife.

Chapter 7: Cultural Experiences

33. Alaska's Indigenous Cultures and History

Alaska's rich tapestry of Indigenous cultures and history is an integral part of the state's identity. Travelers seeking a deeper understanding of Alaska should take the time to explore the traditions, stories, and heritage of its native peoples.

Understanding Alaska's Indigenous Peoples:
Alaska is home to numerous Indigenous groups, each with its own distinct culture, languages, and traditions. Some of the prominent Indigenous groups in Alaska include the Athabascan, Yup'ik, Inupiaq, Tlingit, Haida, and Aleut peoples. Each of these cultures has a unique history, art, and way of life that has been shaped by the land and environment in which they live.

Visiting Cultural Centers and Museums:
To learn about Alaska's Indigenous cultures, consider visiting cultural centers and museums dedicated to preserving and showcasing their heritage. Some notable ones include the Alaska Native Heritage Center in Anchorage, the Inupiat Heritage Center in Barrow, and the Totem Heritage Center in Ketchikan. These places offer interactive

exhibits, traditional art, and opportunities to meet and interact with Indigenous artists and educators.

Traditional Arts and Crafts:
Alaska's Indigenous communities have a rich tradition of art and craftsmanship. You can find beautifully crafted items such as woven baskets, intricately carved totem poles, beaded clothing, and traditional masks. Many local markets and shops sell authentic Indigenous artwork, providing you with an opportunity to support local artisans and bring a piece of Alaska's heritage home with you.

Respect for Indigenous Lands and Customs:
When visiting Indigenous lands and communities, it's essential to show respect for local customs and traditions. Ask for permission before taking photographs, be mindful of sacred sites, and engage with locals in a culturally sensitive way. Many Indigenous communities offer guided tours and cultural experiences that allow travelers to learn directly from the people who call Alaska home.

Alaska's Indigenous Festivals and Events:
If your visit aligns with the timing of local events, consider attending Indigenous festivals and gatherings. These celebrations often feature traditional dances, music, storytelling, and food.

The annual Alaska Federation of Natives Convention is one of the largest gatherings of Indigenous peoples in the state, offering a unique opportunity to immerse yourself in Alaska's Indigenous cultures.

Historical Sites and Landmarks:
Alaska's history is not just about its Indigenous peoples but also includes the Russian colonial period, Gold Rush era, and more. Exploring historical sites like Sitka National Historical Park, where you can see stunning totem poles, or the Kennecott Mines National Historic Landmark, provides insight into Alaska's diverse past.

Alaska's Indigenous cultures and history are an essential part of the state's identity. By taking the time to learn about and respect these cultures, travelers can gain a deeper appreciation for the land, its people, and the unique experiences that await in the Last Frontier. Embrace the opportunity to engage with Alaska's Indigenous communities, and your journey will be both educational and enriching.

34. Museums, Art, and Cultural Centers

Alaska's rich and diverse cultural heritage is on full display in its museums, art galleries, and cultural centers. Exploring these institutions offers travelers a deeper understanding of the state's history, indigenous cultures, and vibrant arts scene.

Museums

1. Alaska Native Heritage Center (Anchorage): Immerse yourself in the traditions and stories of Alaska's indigenous peoples. The center features interactive exhibits, cultural performances, and artisan demonstrations.

2. Alaska State Museum (Juneau): Discover Alaska's history through artifacts, art, and exhibits. Highlights include the Gold Rush era and a fascinating collection of native art.

3. University of Alaska Museum of the North (Fairbanks): This museum showcases the natural and cultural history of Alaska. The impressive collection includes dinosaur fossils, native art, and contemporary Alaskan artists' works.

4. Anchorage Museum at Rasmuson Center (Anchorage): A blend of art, history, and science, this museum houses an extensive collection of Alaskan art and hosts traveling exhibitions that showcase the state's contemporary culture.

Art Galleries

5. Alaska Pacific University Art Galleries (Anchorage): This university's galleries feature a range of contemporary Alaskan art, from paintings to sculptures, providing insight into the thriving local art scene.

6. Fairbanks Arts Association (Fairbanks): Explore the creativity of Alaskan artists through rotating exhibitions of paintings, photography, and other visual arts.

Cultural Centers

7. Alutiiq Museum and Archaeological Repository (Kodiak): Learn about the Alutiiq people and their history through exhibits featuring artifacts, traditional crafts, and storytelling.

8. Doyon, Limited - Athabascan Cultural Center (Fairbanks): Delve into the traditions and lifeways of Alaska's Athabascan people. The center offers demonstrations of traditional activities and hosts cultural events.

9. Ketchikan Totem Heritage Center (Ketchikan): Admire the craftsmanship of totem poles and learn about their cultural significance. This center preserves and educates visitors about indigenous artistry.

10. Sealaska Heritage Institute (Juneau): Dedicated to the cultures of the Tlingit, Haida, and Tsimshian people, this institute promotes and preserves native art, language, and traditions.

Visiting these museums, art galleries, and cultural centers not only provides a glimpse into Alaska's past and present but also supports local artists and the preservation of indigenous cultures. Whether you're interested in history, art, or connecting with the state's native heritage, Alaska has something to offer every curious traveler.

35. Festivals and Events: Celebrating Alaska's Spirit

Alaska is a land of rugged natural beauty and boundless wilderness, but it's also a place where vibrant cultural traditions and celebrations thrive. Throughout the year, the state comes alive with a rich tapestry of festivals and events that offer visitors a unique opportunity to immerse themselves in Alaska's spirit. Here are some of the most captivating festivals and events that you won't want to miss during your visit:

1. Anchorage Fur Rendezvous (Fur Rondy)
   - When: Late February
   - Where: Anchorage
   - Anchorage's Fur Rendezvous is a winter carnival that celebrates Alaska's fur-trading heritage. Visitors can witness exciting events like the World Championship Sled Dog Races, ice carving competitions, and the iconic Running of the Reindeer.

2. Iditarod Trail Sled Dog Race
   - When: Early March
   - Where: Anchorage to Nome
   - Known as "The Last Great Race on Earth," the Iditarod is a 1,000-mile dog sled race from Anchorage to Nome. Attend the ceremonial start in Anchorage or experience the race's thrilling conclusion in Nome.

3. Sitka WhaleFest
   - When: November
   - Where: Sitka
   - Sitka WhaleFest is a marine science festival that combines education with entertainment. Learn about marine life through workshops, lectures, and

even a fun run, all while enjoying the stunning coastal beauty of Sitka.

4. Summer Solstice Celebration
   - When: June 21st
   - Where: Fairbanks
   - Experience the land of the midnight sun during the Summer Solstice Celebration in Fairbanks. Enjoy a variety of outdoor activities, live music, and the Midnight Sun Baseball Game played without artificial lighting.

5. Alaska State Fair
   - When: Late August to early September
   - Where: Palmer
   - The Alaska State Fair is an extravaganza of agriculture, entertainment, and community spirit. Explore giant vegetables, enjoy live concerts, indulge in unique fair foods, and experience the joy of this quintessential Alaskan event.

6. Alaska Native Heritage Center Celebrations
   - When: Various dates
   - Where: Anchorage
   - The Alaska Native Heritage Center in Anchorage hosts a series of events throughout the year, showcasing the rich cultural traditions of Alaska's Indigenous peoples. From traditional dances to art

exhibitions, these events provide a deep insight into Alaska's Indigenous heritage.

7. Kodiak Crab Festival
   - When: Memorial Day Weekend
   - Where: Kodiak
   - Celebrate the arrival of summer in Kodiak with the Crab Festival. Enjoy fresh seafood, carnival rides, live music, and the "Deadliest Catch" crab races, all while soaking in the picturesque coastal atmosphere.

These festivals and events are just a glimpse of the vibrant culture and spirit that Alaska has to offer. They provide a unique opportunity to connect with both the people and the natural wonders of the state, making your Alaska journey even more memorable and meaningful. Be sure to check the dates and plan your trip to coincide with these celebrations for an authentic Alaskan experience.

Chapter 8: Practical Information

36. Transportation Options in Alaska

Alaska, known for its vast wilderness and rugged terrain, offers a variety of transportation options to explore this unique and breathtaking state. Navigating Alaska can be an adventure in itself, and the choice of transportation can greatly impact your experience. Here are some key transportation options to consider when planning your Alaska adventure:

1. Rental Cars: Renting a car is one of the most flexible ways to explore Alaska. You can access remote areas and set your own schedule. Major cities like Anchorage, Fairbanks, and Juneau have rental car agencies, but book in advance, especially during the busy summer season.

2. RVs and Campervans: If you're seeking a mix of transportation and accommodation, renting an RV or campervan is an excellent choice. Alaska has numerous campgrounds, some with stunning views, making it convenient for travelers who want to immerse themselves in the wilderness.

3. Public Transportation: Alaska offers public bus services, such as the Alaska Marine Highway

System (ferry system) and the Alaska Railroad. These are great options for those who prefer not to drive and want to relax while enjoying scenic views.

4. Domestic Flights: Due to its immense size, flying is often the quickest way to cover long distances in Alaska. Airlines like Alaska Airlines and smaller regional carriers connect major cities and remote communities. Be prepared for stunning aerial views during your flights.

5. Cruises: Exploring Alaska via a cruise ship is a popular choice for travelers who want to experience the state's coastal beauty and wildlife. Cruises typically visit coastal cities and fjords, allowing you to see glaciers and marine life up close.

6. Tours and Guided Excursions: Joining guided tours or excursions can be an efficient way to experience Alaska's highlights. Options range from guided bus tours to wilderness adventures like dog sledding or glacier trekking.

7. Bicycles and Hiking: In cities and towns, you can explore by renting a bicycle or simply walking. Many places offer scenic walking trails, and biking is a great way to explore local communities and scenic byways.

8. Taxis and Rideshares: While taxis and rideshares like Uber and Lyft are available in some cities, they may be less common in remote areas. It's advisable to check availability and rates in advance.

9. Boating and Ferries: If you plan to explore Alaska's islands and coastal regions, consider taking a boat tour or using the state's extensive ferry system, known as the Alaska Marine Highway. This is a unique way to experience Alaska's maritime beauty.

10. Snowmobiles and ATVs: In the winter, snowmobiles are a popular mode of transportation, especially in areas with heavy snowfall. Similarly, all-terrain vehicles (ATVs) are used in the warmer months to access remote backcountry areas.

Remember that Alaska's weather and road conditions can vary greatly, so it's essential to plan accordingly, especially if you're driving. Always check for road closures and weather advisories, and be prepared for the unexpected. Whether you choose to explore by land, sea, or air, Alaska's transportation options will help you discover the incredible beauty and wilderness of the Last Frontier.

37. Budgeting and Cost Considerations

Alaska, with its breathtaking landscapes and unique experiences, offers a once-in-a-lifetime adventure. However, it's essential to plan your trip with a clear understanding of the costs involved. While Alaska can be an expensive destination, with thoughtful planning, you can enjoy its wonders without breaking the bank.

1. Transportation Costs:
   - Flights: The cost of flying to Alaska can vary significantly depending on your departure location, time of booking, and the season. Booking in advance and being flexible with travel dates can help you find the best deals.
   - Rental Cars: If you plan to explore Alaska extensively, consider renting a car. Keep in mind that prices can be higher during peak tourist season, so booking early is advisable.

2. Accommodation:
   - Lodging options range from budget-friendly hostels and campgrounds to luxurious lodges. Research and book accommodations in advance, especially during the summer months when demand is high.

- Consider alternative lodging options such as cabins, vacation rentals, and RV parks, which can be more cost-effective for families or groups.

3. Dining:
  - Dining out in Alaska can be expensive, but there are ways to manage costs. Look for local diners and cafes, where you can enjoy reasonably priced meals.
  - Take advantage of happy hour specials and explore food trucks for affordable and delicious options.

4. Activities and Tours:
  - Alaska offers a wide range of activities and tours, from glacier hikes to wildlife cruises. Prioritize your must-do experiences and budget accordingly.
  - Some national parks and wildlife reserves have entrance fees, so factor these into your budget.

5. Miscellaneous Expenses:
  - Souvenirs, gifts, and additional activities can add up quickly. Set aside a discretionary budget for these extras.
  - Always carry some cash, as some remote areas may have limited card payment options.

6. Travel Insurance:

- Travel insurance is essential for your Alaskan adventure. It can protect you from unexpected expenses due to trip cancellations, medical emergencies, or lost luggage.

7. Seasonal Considerations:
   - Traveling during the shoulder seasons (spring and fall) can often lead to cost savings, as prices for accommodations and tours may be lower than during the peak summer months.

8. Discounts and Passes:
   - Look for discounts and passes, such as the Alaska TourSaver book or the Alaska State Parks pass, which can provide significant savings on tours and park entry fees.

9. Plan Ahead:
   - Start budgeting for your Alaska trip well in advance. Create a detailed itinerary and estimate costs for each component.
   - Keep an eye on deals and promotions offered by airlines, hotels, and tour operators.

By carefully considering these budgeting and cost considerations, you can make the most of your Alaska adventure without overspending. With proper planning, you'll be able to savor the stunning landscapes and unique experiences that Alaska has to offer while staying within your budget.

38. Communication and Connectivity

Alaska's breathtaking wilderness may offer unparalleled natural beauty, but it can also present unique challenges when it comes to staying connected and communicating effectively. In this part, we explore the various aspects of communication and connectivity you'll encounter during your Alaskan adventure.

1. Cellular Coverage

Alaska's vast landscapes are not entirely blanketed with cellular coverage. While major cities like Anchorage, Fairbanks, and Juneau boast reliable networks, you may experience gaps in coverage as you venture into remote areas or national parks. It's advisable to check with your cellular provider about coverage maps and options for temporary upgrades if you plan to explore less populated regions.

2. Satellite Phones

For travelers heading deep into the Alaskan wilderness, investing in a satellite phone is a wise choice. These devices rely on satellites for connectivity, ensuring you can make emergency calls or stay in touch with loved ones even in the most remote corners of the state. Be sure to rent or purchase one before embarking on your adventure.

3. Internet Access

Access to the internet varies widely in Alaska. In urban centers, you'll find high-speed Wi-Fi in hotels, cafes, and public spaces. However, in more remote areas, internet access may be limited or slower. Some lodges and accommodations in remote regions may offer limited Wi-Fi, but don't expect the same level of connectivity you're used to in metropolitan areas.

4. Communication in National Parks

When exploring Alaska's national parks, such as Denali, Wrangell-St. Elias, or Glacier Bay, be prepared for limited cell service and internet access. Park facilities may have payphones for emergency use, but it's essential to plan ahead and inform someone of your itinerary if you're venturing deep into these pristine wilderness areas.

5. Two-Way Radios

For group travel or backcountry adventures, consider using two-way radios. These devices can be essential for staying connected with your travel companions when out of cellular range. They provide an effective means of communication, especially when hiking, camping, or navigating remote terrain.

6. Emergency Communication

Safety is a top priority in Alaska's wild landscapes. Familiarize yourself with emergency contact numbers, such as Alaska State Troopers, the U.S. Coast Guard, or local search and rescue teams. In case of an emergency, these organizations can provide assistance, even in remote areas.

7. Paper Maps and GPS

Always carry paper maps, especially if you plan to explore off-the-beaten-path regions. GPS devices are useful, but they can fail in extreme conditions. A good old-fashioned map can be a lifesaver if your electronic devices falter.

In Alaska, connectivity and communication may not always be seamless, but that's part of the adventure. Embrace the opportunity to disconnect from the digital world and immerse yourself in the stunning natural surroundings. Prioritize safety, plan your communications strategy, and savor the moments of true wilderness that Alaska offers.

39. Health and Safety Tips

Alaska's stunning wilderness and rugged landscapes offer unparalleled opportunities for adventure, but it's important to prioritize your health and safety during your visit. Here are essential health and safety tips to keep in mind when exploring the Last Frontier:

1. Weather Awareness: Alaska's weather can be unpredictable. Pack and dress in layers to adapt to changing conditions. Be prepared for rain, snow, and sun, sometimes all in the same day. Check weather forecasts regularly, especially if you're embarking on outdoor activities.

2. Wildlife Encounter Safety: Alaska is home to diverse wildlife, including bears, moose, and wolves. Familiarize yourself with wildlife safety guidelines, such as carrying bear spray, making noise on trails, and storing food properly to avoid attracting animals to your campsite.

3. Hypothermia Prevention: Even during summer, Alaska's temperatures can drop rapidly. Hypothermia is a real concern. Wear appropriate clothing, stay dry, and know the signs of hypothermia, which include shivering, confusion, and drowsiness.

4. Stay Hydrated: Dehydration can occur in Alaska's dry, high-altitude regions. Always carry water and drink regularly, especially when engaged in physical activities.

5. Sun Protection: Sunburn can be severe in Alaska due to the angle of the sun. Use sunscreen with high SPF, wear sunglasses, and don't forget a wide-brimmed hat.

6. Respect Local Customs: Alaska has a rich indigenous culture. Respect local customs and traditions, and seek permission before entering private lands or tribal areas.

7. Water Safety: If you plan to go boating or kayaking, wear a life jacket, and be aware of water conditions and tides. Alaska's waters can be frigid, so be prepared for cold-water immersion.

8. Road Safety: If you're driving in Alaska, be cautious of wildlife on the roads, particularly at dawn and dusk. Follow road signs, and be prepared for long distances between gas stations.

9. Emergency Preparedness: Familiarize yourself with local emergency contact numbers and the nearest medical facilities. Carry a basic first-aid kit and know how to use it.

10. Bear Safety: When in bear country, make noise, travel in groups, and carry bear spray. Learn about the different types of bears in Alaska and how to respond if you encounter one.

11. Food Safety: Properly store and prepare food to prevent foodborne illnesses. Dispose of trash in bear-proof containers or as directed by local authorities.

12. Leave No Trace: Follow the principles of Leave No Trace ethics, which include packing out all trash and minimizing your impact on the environment.

13. Travel Insurance: Consider purchasing travel insurance that covers emergency medical expenses and trip cancellations. Medical care in remote areas can be expensive.

14. Altitude Considerations: Some parts of Alaska are at high altitudes. If you have pre-existing health conditions, consult your doctor before visiting high-altitude areas.

By following these health and safety tips, you can fully enjoy the beauty and adventure that Alaska offers while minimizing risks and ensuring a memorable and safe journey in the Last Frontier. Always remember that safety should be a top priority when exploring this magnificent but challenging terrain.

40. Sustainable Travel in Alaska

Alaska's pristine natural beauty and diverse ecosystems are among its greatest treasures. To ensure that these treasures remain for generations to come, it's important to practice sustainable travel when exploring the Last Frontier. Sustainable travel in Alaska not only helps protect the environment but also respects the rich cultural heritage of the state's indigenous communities.

Responsible Outdoor Adventures:

1. Leave No Trace: Follow the Leave No Trace principles when hiking, camping, or engaging in

outdoor activities. Pack out everything you bring in, dispose of waste properly, and minimize your impact on fragile ecosystems.

2. Responsible Wildlife Viewing: Keep a safe and respectful distance from wildlife. Use binoculars or telephoto lenses to observe animals, and never feed them. Admire these creatures from afar and allow them to roam freely.

Choosing Sustainable Accommodations:

3. Eco-Friendly Lodging: Look for eco-certified accommodations that prioritize sustainable practices such as energy conservation, waste reduction, and water preservation. Many lodges and hotels in Alaska are committed to reducing their carbon footprint.

Respecting Local Communities:

4. Support Indigenous Tourism: Engage in cultural experiences offered by Alaska's indigenous communities. These experiences provide insight into the rich traditions and history of Alaska's native peoples while contributing to their economic well-being.

5. Buy Local: Purchase souvenirs and goods from local artisans and businesses. This supports the local economy and reduces the environmental impact of shipping products from afar.

Sustainable Transportation:

6. Public Transit and Carpooling: In cities like Anchorage and Fairbanks, consider using public transportation or carpooling to reduce emissions. Alaska's vast size often necessitates driving, so opt for fuel-efficient vehicles and plan your routes efficiently.

7. Take the Train: Alaska Railroad offers scenic train journeys that not only provide an eco-friendly mode of transportation but also showcase stunning landscapes.

Waste Reduction:

8. Recycle and Reuse: Practice recycling and reuse wherever possible. Alaska has recycling facilities in many towns, so make use of them to reduce waste.

9. Single-Use Plastics: Avoid single-use plastics like water bottles and shopping bags. Carry a reusable water bottle and bring your own shopping bags.

Responsible Fishing and Seafood Dining:

10. Responsible Fishing: If you plan to fish in Alaska, understand and follow local fishing regulations to protect fish populations. Catch-and-release practices can help preserve the ecosystem.

11. Sustainable Seafood: When dining out, choose restaurants that serve sustainable seafood. Alaska is known for its delicious seafood, and supporting sustainable fishing practices is essential for the state's fisheries.

Leave a Positive Impact:

12. Participate in Cleanup Efforts: Join local conservation organizations in cleanup activities. Alaska's vast coastline and wilderness areas benefit greatly from volunteer efforts to keep them clean.

By practicing sustainable travel in Alaska, you can enjoy its natural wonders while helping to conserve its environment and support its communities. Responsible travel ensures that future generations can continue to experience the magnificence of the Last Frontier.

Chapter 9: Itineraries and Sample Plans

41. One-Week Itinerary for a Family Adventure

Day 1: Arrival in Anchorage
- Arrive in Anchorage, Alaska's largest city.
- Check into your family-friendly accommodation.
- Explore downtown Anchorage, visit the Anchorage Museum, and enjoy a meal at a local restaurant.

Day 2: Anchorage Outdoor Fun
- Start your day with a visit to the Alaska Wildlife Conservation Center.
- Afternoon trip to the Alaska Zoo, perfect for kids.
- Evening stroll along the scenic Tony Knowles Coastal Trail.

Day 3: Denali National Park
- Drive or take a scenic train ride to Denali National Park.
- Check into a lodge near the park entrance.
- Enjoy an evening wildlife tour or a relaxing campfire.

Day 4: Denali Adventure
- Take a bus tour deep into Denali National Park.

- Look for wildlife, including grizzly bears, moose, and caribou.
- Learn about the park's natural history and geology.

Day 5: Fairbanks and Northern Lights
- Drive to Fairbanks, known for its unique culture.
- Visit the Museum of the North and Pioneer Park.
- In the evening, chase the Northern Lights (seasonal) or enjoy a dog sledding experience.

Day 6: Arctic Adventure
- Take a day trip to the Arctic Circle by guided tour.
- Witness the stark beauty of Alaska's far north.
- Learn about the culture of the Inupiaq Eskimos.

Day 7: Return to Anchorage
- Drive or fly back to Anchorage.
- Spend your last day shopping for souvenirs in downtown Anchorage.
- Reflect on your family adventure with a farewell dinner.

This one-week family adventure itinerary combines outdoor experiences, wildlife encounters, and cultural exploration, making it a memorable trip for all ages. Be sure to check the seasonal availability of activities and accommodations, as Alaska's climate can vary throughout the year.

42. Two-Week Solo Expedition

Day 1-3: Anchorage - Gateway to the North
- Arrive in Anchorage, Alaska's largest city.
- Explore the Anchorage Museum and enjoy local cuisine.
- Take a scenic flightseeing tour over the Chugach Mountains.
- Hike in Chugach State Park.

Day 4-6: Denali National Park - Wilderness Encounter
- Drive or take a bus to Denali National Park.
- Spend two days exploring the park's wilderness.
- Go wildlife viewing, hiking, or take a guided tour.
- Enjoy the stunning vistas of Denali (Mount McKinley).

Day 7-8: Fairbanks - Northern Lights and History
- Drive to Fairbanks, Alaska's second-largest city.
- Visit the Museum of the North and learn about the region's history.
- At night, chase the Northern Lights (Aurora Borealis).

Day 9-11: The Arctic Region - Untamed Beauty

- Fly to the Arctic region, such as Barrow or Nome.
- Explore the Arctic tundra, visit local communities, and learn about Inupiaq culture.
- Witness the midnight sun (depending on the season).
- Take a dip in the Arctic Ocean (for the brave!).

Day 12-14: Southeast Alaska - Rainforests and Glaciers
- Fly to Juneau, Alaska's capital in the southeast.
- Explore Tongass National Forest, a temperate rainforest.
- Visit Mendenhall Glacier and go whale watching.
- Take a ferry or cruise through the Inside Passage to Ketchikan.
- Explore Ketchikan's rich Native American heritage and totem poles.

End of Expedition: Return to Anchorage for Departure

This two-week solo expedition takes you through the diverse landscapes of Alaska, from the urban hub of Anchorage to the wild beauty of Denali, the far reaches of the Arctic, and the lush rainforests of Southeast Alaska. It offers a balanced mix of adventure, culture, and natural wonders, making it an unforgettable journey for solo travelers seeking the best of Alaska's wilderness and culture.

43. *Romantic Escape in Alaska: a 5-Day Plan*

Day 1: Arrival in Anchorage
- Arrive at Ted Stevens Anchorage International Airport.
- Check into a cozy cabin or boutique hotel in Anchorage.
- Enjoy a leisurely dinner at a local seafood restaurant overlooking the water.
- Take a romantic evening stroll along the Tony Knowles Coastal Trail.

Day 2: Exploring Anchorage
- Have breakfast at a charming cafe in downtown Anchorage.
- Visit the Anchorage Museum at Rasmuson Center to explore Alaskan art and culture.
- In the afternoon, take a scenic drive to Chugach State Park for a short hike.
- Dine at a fine dining restaurant in Anchorage.

Day 3: Journey to Girdwood
- Check out of your Anchorage accommodation.
- Drive south to the picturesque town of Girdwood.

- Visit the Alaska Wildlife Conservation Center en route.
- Check into a romantic lodge or cabin in Girdwood.
- Enjoy dinner at a restaurant known for its mountain views.

Day 4: Adventure in Girdwood
- Take the Alyeska Aerial Tram for breathtaking views of the surrounding mountains.
- Spend the day hiking or biking in the Chugach Mountains.
- Relax at the Alyeska Resort's spa in the afternoon.
- Have a romantic dinner at a mountaintop restaurant.

Day 5: Kenai Fjords National Park Cruise
- Drive to Seward, a charming coastal town.
- Embark on a Kenai Fjords National Park cruise to witness glaciers and wildlife.
- Enjoy a picnic lunch on board.
- Return to Seward and savor a fresh seafood dinner.
- Spend the night at a waterfront lodge in Seward.

Day 6: Departure
- Enjoy a leisurely breakfast in Seward.
- Visit the Alaska SeaLife Center before leaving.

- Drive back to Anchorage or continue your Alaskan adventure.

This 5-day itinerary provides a mix of adventure, relaxation, and romantic experiences in Alaska, from exploring Anchorage's cultural scene to enjoying the stunning natural beauty of Girdwood and Kenai Fjords National Park. It's designed to create memorable moments for couples seeking a romantic escape in the Last Frontier.

44. *Customizing Your Alaska Experience*

Alaska is a vast and diverse land, offering a multitude of experiences for travelers. One of the most exciting aspects of planning your Alaska journey is the ability to customize it to match your interests, preferences, and sense of adventure. Whether you're a solo traveler seeking solitude, a family looking for kid-friendly activities, or a couple yearning for a romantic escape, Alaska has something unique to offer. Here are some tips on how to tailor your Alaskan adventure:

1. Choose Your Adventure Type:
   - Wilderness Exploration: If you're an outdoor enthusiast, consider a rugged journey into Alaska's wilderness. Plan hikes, camping trips, and wildlife encounters.

- Cultural Immersion: For a more cultural experience, focus on visiting museums, indigenous heritage sites, and attending local festivals.
- Relaxation and Romance: Couples can opt for secluded cabins, scenic drives, and intimate dining experiences to create a romantic atmosphere.
- Family Fun: Families should prioritize child-friendly activities such as wildlife safaris, nature centers, and interactive museums.

2. Pick Your Ideal Season:
   - Summer (June to August): Perfect for hiking, fishing, and enjoying long daylight hours.
   - Fall (September to October): Witness the breathtaking fall foliage and enjoy fewer crowds.
   - Winter (November to March): Ideal for snow sports and witnessing the Northern Lights.
   - Spring (April to May): A quieter time to explore, with budding flora and emerging wildlife.

3. Plan Your Itinerary:
   - Research Alaska's diverse regions, from the bustling Anchorage to the remote Arctic wilderness. Choose destinations that align with your interests.
   - Create a day-by-day itinerary, balancing adventure with relaxation and taking into account any family-specific needs.

4. Accommodation Choices:
   - Alaska offers a range of accommodations, from luxury lodges to rustic cabins and campgrounds. Match your lodging to your travel style and budget.

5. Activities and Tours:
   - Book tours and activities in advance, especially for popular attractions like Denali National Park or glacier cruises. Be sure to inquire about age restrictions for kids.

6. Dining Preferences:
   - Explore Alaska's diverse cuisine, from fresh seafood to indigenous dishes. Make reservations if you're planning a special dining experience.

7. Pack Accordingly:
   - Prepare for Alaska's variable weather by packing layers, waterproof gear, and essential outdoor equipment based on your planned activities.

8. Travel Responsibly:
   - Respect local wildlife and follow Leave No Trace principles to minimize your impact on the environment.

9. Be Flexible:

- Alaska's weather can be unpredictable, so have backup plans in case of adverse conditions. Embrace the spontaneity of your journey.

10. Capture Memories:
- Bring a camera or smartphone to capture the breathtaking landscapes and unique moments you'll encounter.

Remember, your Alaska experience is a personal journey. Customize it to suit your interests, and don't hesitate to ask locals or tour operators for advice and recommendations. Whether you're traveling solo, with family, or as a couple, Alaska's untamed beauty and boundless adventure await your exploration.

Chapter 10: Resources and Contacts

45. Useful Websites and Apps

As you embark on your Alaskan adventure, you'll find that technology can be a valuable companion, helping you navigate, plan, and make the most of your trip. Here's a list of websites and apps that will prove indispensable during your journey through the Last Frontier:

1. Alaska Travel Official Website (travelalaska.com)
   - The official tourism website for Alaska is a treasure trove of information. You'll find travel tips, itineraries, and updates on local events and attractions.

2. Alaska Airlines Mobile App
   - If you're flying to Alaska, the Alaska Airlines app is handy for booking flights, managing reservations, and checking in. It also provides real-time flight information.

3. Weather Apps
   - Alaska's weather can be unpredictable. Download weather apps like Weather.com, The Weather Channel, or AccuWeather to stay informed about local conditions and forecasts.

4. AllTrails
   - Hiking enthusiasts will love AllTrails. It offers detailed trail maps, reviews, and user-generated photos, making it easy to choose the perfect hiking route.

5. Alaska's State Parks App
   - For those planning to explore Alaska's state parks, this app provides information on park locations, activities, and camping options.

6. Alaska Map App
   - To navigate Alaska's vast landscapes, consider a mapping app like Google Maps, which can be used offline, or Gaia GPS for detailed topographical maps.

7. Aurora Forecast Apps
   - If witnessing the Northern Lights is on your bucket list, apps like Aurora Forecast and My Aurora Forecast can help you track aurora borealis activity and find optimal viewing locations.

8. Alaska Wildlife Viewing App
   - Designed for wildlife enthusiasts, this app helps you locate and identify Alaska's diverse wildlife. It includes tips on responsible wildlife viewing.

9. GasBuddy
   - If you're driving in Alaska, GasBuddy can help you find the nearest and most affordable gas stations along your route.

10. Yelp and TripAdvisor
    - When it comes to dining and accommodations, Yelp and TripAdvisor are valuable for reading reviews and recommendations from fellow travelers.

11. The Alaska App
    - This comprehensive app offers information on attractions, accommodations, restaurants, and local events. It's a great all-in-one resource for travelers.

12. Alaska Department of Transportation (DOT) 511 App
    - For road condition updates and real-time traffic information, the DOT 511 app is essential for road trippers.

13. Wildlife Alert Reporting Program (WARP)
    - Use this app to report wildlife sightings and contribute to citizen science efforts in Alaska.

These websites and apps are just a few of the digital tools available to enhance your Alaska travel experience. Remember to download them before your trip, ensure offline functionality where needed, and let technology be your guide while you explore this stunning and diverse state.

46. Emergency Contacts and Services

While Alaska offers breathtaking natural beauty and thrilling adventures, it's important to be prepared for unexpected situations during your trip. Familiarizing yourself with emergency contacts and services is essential to ensure your safety and well-being throughout your journey in the Last Frontier.

1. Emergency Services:

- 911: In the case of life-threatening emergencies, dial 911 for immediate assistance. This number connects you to local law enforcement, medical services, and fire departments.

2. Medical Facilities:

- Hospitals and Clinics: Alaska has well-equipped medical facilities, especially in major cities like Anchorage, Fairbanks, and Juneau. Look for the nearest hospital or clinic in your area if you require medical attention.

3. Search and Rescue:

- Alaska State Troopers: They handle search and rescue operations across the state. In remote areas, contact the nearest trooper post for assistance.

4. Coast Guard:

- United States Coast Guard: For maritime emergencies, contact the Coast Guard. Alaska's coastline is extensive, and they are responsible for water-based rescues.

5. Air Ambulance Services:

- LifeMed Alaska: This organization provides air ambulance services across the state, particularly in remote areas where access to medical facilities is limited.

6. Roadside Assistance:

- Alaska Department of Transportation and Public Facilities (DOT&PF): In case of vehicle breakdowns on major highways, you can call DOT&PF for assistance. Keep in mind that some remote areas may not have immediate access to services.

7. Wildlife Encounters:

- Alaska Department of Fish and Game: If you encounter wildlife-related issues or emergencies, such as aggressive bears, contact the local Fish and Game office for guidance.

8. Weather and Avalanche Information:

- National Weather Service: For weather-related concerns and avalanche warnings, stay updated with the National Weather Service forecasts and alerts.

9. Travel Advisories:

- Alaska Department of Transportation and Public Facilities (DOT&PF): Check for road closures, weather-related travel advisories, and real-time road conditions on the DOT&PF website before embarking on your journey.

10. Lost and Found:

- Alaska State Troopers: If you lose valuables or need assistance with lost items, contact the Alaska State Troopers or local law enforcement.

Remember that Alaska's vast and rugged terrain can present unique challenges. It's advisable to inform someone about your travel plans, especially if you're venturing into remote areas. Additionally, having a well-stocked emergency kit, including essentials like food, water, first aid supplies, and communication devices, can be invaluable in unforeseen circumstances.

Safety should always be a top priority when exploring Alaska's wild landscapes, and being prepared with the right emergency contacts and services will help ensure a memorable and secure journey in this remarkable destination.

47. *Travel Agencies and Tour Operators*

Alaska offers an awe-inspiring natural landscape and a wide array of activities for travelers to enjoy, but planning a trip here can be quite complex due to its vastness and unique challenges. Travel agencies and tour operators in Alaska play a vital role in helping visitors make the most of their experience. Whether you're a solo traveler, a family with kids, or a couple seeking adventure, these experts can enhance your journey in several ways.

Why Use Travel Agencies and Tour Operators?

1. Local Expertise: Alaska-based travel agencies and tour operators possess in-depth knowledge of the region. They can guide you to hidden gems, offer insights into local cultures, and suggest the best times to visit specific attractions.

2. Customized Itineraries: Depending on your preferences, these professionals can create personalized itineraries. Whether you're interested in wildlife encounters, outdoor adventures, or cultural experiences, they can tailor a plan to meet your desires.

3. Logistics and Transportation: Navigating Alaska's vast wilderness can be challenging. Travel agencies can arrange transportation, including flights, trains, and cruises, to ensure you get where you need to be comfortably and efficiently.

4. Group Tours: For those who prefer to travel with others, group tours organized by tour operators are a fantastic option. These tours often provide an instant social network of fellow travelers.

5. Safety and Peace of Mind: Alaska's rugged terrain and wildlife require careful planning. Travel agencies ensure your safety by offering guided tours

with experienced leaders who know how to handle any unexpected situations.

Types of Tours Offered

1. Wildlife Tours: Alaska is renowned for its diverse wildlife, including bears, whales, and eagles. Tour operators can arrange wildlife-focused excursions, such as bear viewing trips or whale-watching cruises.

2. Adventure Tours: Thrill-seekers can opt for adventure tours, which may include activities like kayaking, glacier hiking, and dog sledding.

3. Cultural Tours: Immerse yourself in Alaska's rich indigenous cultures by joining cultural tours that visit native villages, art galleries, and heritage sites.

4. Cruises: Explore Alaska's stunning coastline and fjords on a cruise. Travel agencies can help you choose the right cruise line and itinerary for your preferences.

5. Northern Lights Tours: Witness the mesmerizing Northern Lights in the Arctic region with specialized tours that maximize your chances of seeing this natural wonder.

Choosing a Travel Agency or Tour Operator

When selecting a travel agency or tour operator in Alaska, consider the following:

- Reputation: Look for agencies with positive reviews and a good reputation for customer service.

- Certifications: Ensure they are licensed and certified by relevant authorities, such as the Alaska Travel Industry Association.

- Flexibility: Check if they can tailor packages to suit your specific interests and needs.

- Inclusivity: Confirm that they accommodate different types of travelers, whether you're solo, a family, or a couple.

- Price: Compare prices and inclusions to find the best value for your budget.

Alaska's travel agencies and tour operators can turn your visit into an unforgettable adventure. Their expertise and local knowledge ensure that you make the most of your time in this captivating and rugged destination. Whether you're exploring glaciers, encountering wildlife, or delving into indigenous cultures, these professionals are your gateway to the wonders of the Last Frontier.

Appendices

- Packing Checklist

One of the keys to a successful trip to Alaska is packing the right gear and clothing. The weather can vary significantly depending on the season and region, so it's essential to be prepared for a range of conditions. Here's a comprehensive packing checklist to help you make the most of your Alaskan adventure:

1. Clothing:

- Layered Clothing: The key to staying comfortable in Alaska is layering. Bring base layers, insulating layers, and a waterproof outer layer.
- Waterproof Jacket: A good-quality waterproof and windproof jacket is a must, even in the summer.
- Insulated Jacket: For colder days and evenings.
- Warm Sweaters or Fleece: Pack a few warm layers for chilly evenings.
- Waterproof Pants: Necessary for outdoor activities like hiking and kayaking.
- Convertible Pants: These are handy for changing weather conditions.
- Hiking Boots: Sturdy, waterproof boots with good traction.

- Comfortable Shoes: For city exploration and casual outings.
- Warm Socks and Gloves: Don't underestimate the importance of warm extremities.
- Hat and Sunglasses: Protection from both sun and cold.

2. Outdoor Gear:

- Backpack: For day trips and hikes.
- Trekking Poles: Useful for challenging hikes.
- Binoculars: To spot wildlife from a distance.
- Mosquito Repellent: Especially important in summer.
- Sunscreen: Even on overcast days, UV rays can be strong.

3. Travel Essentials:

- Travel Adapters: Alaska uses Type A and Type B outlets.
- Camera and Extra Batteries: Capture the stunning landscapes.
- Reusable Water Bottle: Access to fresh water is abundant.
- First Aid Kit: Basic supplies for minor injuries.
- Maps and Guidebooks: Handy for navigation and planning.

- Identification and Travel Documents: Passport, visa, driver's license, and copies.
- Cash and Credit Cards: While cards are widely accepted, it's wise to carry some cash.
- Travel Insurance: Ensure you're covered for emergencies.

4. Camping and Adventure Equipment (if applicable):

- Tent, Sleeping Bag, and Sleeping Pad: For camping adventures.
- Cooking Gear: If you plan to cook your meals.
- Bear-Resistant Food Containers: Required in some areas to store food safely.

5. Personal Items:

- Toiletries: Toothbrush, toothpaste, soap, etc.
- Medications: Any prescription or over-the-counter meds you may need.
- Glasses/Contacts: If you wear them.
- Entertainment: Books, e-readers, or other forms of entertainment for downtime.
- Travel Pillow: Useful for long journeys.

6. Miscellaneous:

- Plastic Bags: For keeping items dry and separating dirty laundry.
- Insect Head Net: Handy in mosquito-prone areas.
- Small Travel Sewing Kit: For quick repairs.
- Snacks: High-energy snacks for hikes and long drives.

Remember that Alaska's weather can change rapidly, so it's better to over prepare than underprepared. Check the specific weather forecasts for your destinations and activities before you go, and adjust your packing list accordingly. With the right gear, you'll be well-equipped to explore the stunning landscapes and unique experiences that Alaska has to offer.

- Wildlife Identification Guide

Alaska is renowned for its diverse and abundant wildlife. Whether you're a seasoned wildlife enthusiast or simply looking to appreciate the natural beauty of the state, having a basic understanding of the creatures you might encounter can enhance your Alaskan experience. Here's a guide to some of the iconic wildlife you might spot in Alaska:

1. Bald Eagle (Haliaeetus leucocephalus):

- Description: Large, distinctive white head and tail, dark brown body, and yellow beak.
   - Habitat: Found near coastal areas, lakes, and rivers.
   - Best Viewing Spots: Coastal regions, like Homer and the Kenai Fjords.

2. Brown Bear (Ursus arctos horribilis):
   - Description: Massive brown fur, hump on its back, and a distinctive shoulder hump.
   - Habitat: Coastal areas, forests, and rivers.
   - Best Viewing Spots: Katmai National Park, Lake Clark National Park, and Kodiak Island.

3. Moose (Alces alces):
   - Description: Towering with long legs, a humped shoulder, and broad, flat antlers (in males).
   - Habitat: Forested areas, wetlands, and lakeshores.
   - Best Viewing Spots: Anchorage's Chugach State Park, Denali National Park, and Kenai Peninsula.

4. Humpback Whale (Megaptera novaeangliae):
   - Description: Large, streamlined body with a humpbacked appearance and long pectoral fins.
   - Habitat: Coastal waters, especially during the summer months.

- Best Viewing Spots: Inside Passage, Glacier Bay National Park, and Seward.

5. Dall Sheep (Ovis dalli):
   - Description: White fur, curved horns (in males), and a stocky build.
   - Habitat: Rugged, mountainous terrain.
   - Best Viewing Spots: Denali National Park and Wrangell-St. Elias National Park.

6. Orca (Orcinus orca):
   - Description: Black and white coloring with a distinctive dorsal fin.
   - Habitat: Coastal waters and fjords.
   - Best Viewing Spots: Inside Passage, Resurrection Bay, and Prince William Sound.

7. Salmon:
   - Description: Various species, including sockeye, coho, and king salmon, with different colors and sizes.
   - Habitat: Spawning in rivers and migrating to the ocean.
   - Best Viewing Spots: Brooks Falls (Katmai), Russian River (Kenai Peninsula), and many rivers across the state.

8. Puffins:

- Description: Small seabirds with colorful beaks, including horned and tufted puffins.
   - Habitat: Coastal cliffs and islands.
   - Best Viewing Spots: Kenai Fjords National Park, Pribilof Islands, and Kodiak Island.

9. Wolves (Canis lupus):
   - Description: Gray or black fur, slender bodies, and a keen sense of smell.
   - Habitat: Forests and tundra.
   - Best Viewing Spots: Denali National Park and Yellowstone River Valley.

10. Sea Otter (Enhydra lutris):
   - Description: Brown fur, webbed feet, and a distinctive floating posture.
   - Habitat: Coastal waters, particularly in kelp forests.
   - Best Viewing Spots: Prince William Sound, Glacier Bay, and Kachemak Bay.

Remember to keep a respectful distance from wildlife, use binoculars or a telephoto lens for close-up views, and follow all park regulations to ensure both your safety and the animals' well-being. Observing Alaska's incredible wildlife in its natural habitat is an unforgettable part of any visit to the Last Frontier.

- *Glossary of Alaskan Terms*

Alaska, known for its rugged wilderness and unique culture, has a lexicon all its own. While you explore the Last Frontier, you might encounter terms and phrases that are distinctive to the state. This glossary will help you decode some of the Alaskan terminology you may come across during your journey:

1. Bush: Refers to remote and rural areas of Alaska, often inaccessible by road.

2. Mushing: The act of driving a dog sled team, a cherished Alaskan tradition.

3. Northern Lights: The mesmerizing natural phenomenon also known as the Aurora Borealis, which lights up the night skies in northern Alaska.

4. Iditarod: A world-famous long-distance sled dog race from Anchorage to Nome, held annually.

5. PFD: The Permanent Fund Dividend, an annual payment to Alaska residents from the state's oil revenue.

6. Salmon Run: The migration of salmon from the ocean to their spawning grounds in freshwater streams and rivers.

7. Tundra: Vast, treeless areas of Alaska characterized by low vegetation, often found in the Arctic regions.

8. Boreal Forest: The northern coniferous forest that covers much of interior Alaska.

9. Pioneer: A term used to describe early settlers who played a significant role in Alaska's history.

10. Homesteading: The practice of claiming and developing land in Alaska, a part of its unique land ownership history.

11. Polar Bear Plunge: Taking a dip in frigid Alaskan waters, usually as a challenge or for fun.

12. Eskimo Ice Cream: Also known as "Akutaq," it's a traditional Alaskan dessert made from berries, fat, and sometimes fish.

13. Totem Pole: Carved wooden sculptures that represent indigenous Alaskan cultures and their stories.

14. King Crab: A prized seafood delicacy in Alaska, known for its sweet and tender meat.

15. Mat-Su Valley: Short for the Matanuska-Susitna Valley, a scenic region known for its agriculture and outdoor recreation.

16. Tlingit, Haida, and Tsimshian: Indigenous peoples of Southeast Alaska, each with their unique cultures and languages.

17. Dipnetting: A fishing method where individuals use large nets to catch salmon along the shores of certain Alaskan rivers.

18. Fjord: A long, narrow inlet with steep sides or cliffs, often with glaciers at the head, common in coastal Alaska.

19. Sourdough: A term originally used for old-timer Alaskans, now often referring to a type of pancake or bread made with fermented dough.

20. Subsistence Hunting and Fishing: The practice of hunting and fishing for personal and community sustenance, an important way of life for many Alaskans.

Understanding these terms will not only enrich your Alaskan experience but also help you connect with the unique history and culture of this magnificent state. Embrace these words, and you'll find yourself feeling more at home in the heart of Alaska.

- Recommended Reading and Films

When preparing for your journey to Alaska, immersing yourself in literature and cinema that capture the spirit of this rugged and awe-inspiring land can enhance your appreciation of the state's unique charm. Here are some recommended books and films that will help you connect with Alaska before and during your trip:

Books:

1. Into the Wild by Jon Krakauer: This gripping non-fiction book tells the story of Christopher McCandless, who ventured into the Alaskan wilderness. It's a thought-provoking exploration of the allure and challenges of Alaska's wild places.

2. Alaska by James A. Michener: A classic epic novel that traces the history of Alaska from prehistoric times to the modern era. It offers a deep and comprehensive understanding of the state's complex past.

3. The Call of the Wild by Jack London: A timeless adventure novel set in the Klondike Gold Rush era of the late 19th century. It evokes the untamed wilderness of Alaska and the bond between humans and sled dogs.

4. Two in the Far North by Margaret E. Murie: An autobiographical account of Margaret Murie's life in Alaska, where she became a passionate conservationist. Her vivid descriptions of Alaska's wildlife and landscapes are captivating.

5. Coming into the Country by John McPhee: This non-fiction work delves into the lives of Alaskans in various regions, offering insights into the state's diverse cultures and landscapes.

Films:

1. Into the Wild (2007): Directed by Sean Penn and based on Jon Krakauer's book, this film tells the

story of Christopher McCandless's journey into the Alaskan wilderness. It beautifully captures Alaska's stunning scenery.

2. Wildlike (2014): A touching drama that follows a troubled teenage girl on a hike through the Alaskan wilderness. It showcases both the beauty and challenges of the state's backcountry.

3. Grizzly Man (2005): A documentary by Werner Herzog that explores the life of Timothy Treadwell, who spent years living among grizzly bears in Alaska. It's a fascinating, if cautionary, tale of human-wildlife interaction.

4. Balto (1995): An animated film inspired by the true story of a sled dog hero who helped save the children of Nome during a diphtheria outbreak in 1925. A heartwarming and family-friendly choice.

5. The Grey (2011): A thrilling survival drama starring Liam Neeson as an oil worker stranded in the Alaskan wilderness after a plane crash. It portrays the harshness of Alaska's winters and the struggle for survival.

These books and films offer diverse perspectives on Alaska, from its natural beauty and challenges to the unique stories of those who have explored its wild landscapes. Whether you're seeking inspiration, knowledge, or simply entertainment, these recommendations will enrich your Alaska experience.

Printed in Great Britain
by Amazon